W9-ASN-063

IN-TIME PARENTAL INTERVENTION IS THE BEST WAY TO STOP SUBSTANCE ABUSE

"A child is a person who is going to carry on what you have started He is going to sit where you are sitting, and when you are gone, attend to those things you think are important. You may adopt all of the policies you please, but how they are carried out depends on him. He will assume control of your cities, states, and nations. He is going to move in and take over your houses of worship, schools, universities, and corporations. The fate of humanity is in his hands."

Abraham Lincoln

"The most effective deterrents to alcohol and other drug use among kids aren't the police, or prisons, or politicians. The most effective deterrents are a child's parents. Kids who learn about the risks of using drug and alcohol from parents who know what they are talking about, are far less likely to become users."

Office of National Drug Control Policy

DO <u>YOU</u> KNOW THE FACTS?

DEDICATED TO OUR OWN FAMILY:
Michael and Vicki Van Ost; Lynn Van Ost, Karen Manfre,
Jane and Paul Hansen; Bill and SusannaYoumans;
Jim and Liz Youmans;
and to our grandchildren:
Meagan, Paul and Adrianne Van Ost;
Erik, Caighla and Travis Hansen; Will Youmans;
AND TO ALL FAMILIES OF THE FUTURE.

ABOUT THE AUTHORS

William C. Van Ost, M.D., F.A.A.P. is a Fellow of the American Academy of Pediatrics and a past President of its New Jersey Chapter. After twenty-eight years in the private practice of pediatrics, during which he became aware of the destructive effects of family addiction on his young patients and their families, Dr. Van Ost, seeking to fulfill a need to address the problem, chose to change the direction of his career in 1983 and became a Co-Founder, with his wife, Elaine, of the Van Ost Institute for Family Living, Inc., an outpatient addiction treatment center located in Englewood, New Jersey. A certified member of the American Society of Addiction Medicine, he served for many years as the Institute's Executive Director and Medical Director. He is still active as a Consultant at the Institute and authors a weekly column, "Ask Dr. Bill," for local newspapers and the Institute's web-site. (www.vanostinstitute.org)

Elaine Van Ost, Co-Founder, with her husband, of the Van Ost Institute For Family Living, Inc., served for many years as its Director, involved in its day-by-day management. An active participant in the Institute's marketing and development programs, she has provided essential outreach services; authoring its press releases and has appeared frequently on radio and TV. Her service to the Institute continues, both as a Consultant, involved in its outreach and public relations projects, and as an essential member of its Board of Trustees. A former commercial artist, she maintains her interest in this field through support of the Institute's art therapy programs.

WARNING SIGNS

A PARENT'S GUIDE TO

IN - TIME INTERVENTION IN

DRUG AND

ALCOHOL ABUSE

William C. Van Ost, M.D., F.A.A.P., and Elaine Van Ost, *Co-Founders,*
Van Ost Institute For Family Living, Inc.

Introduction by Donald Ian Macdonald,. M.D.,F.A.A.P.
Former Director, White House Drug Policy Office and
Special Assistant to former President Reagan

Chapter 10 Revised by William Carlos, Jr., M.A., L.P.C.
Executive Director, Van Ost Institute For Family Living

The Van Ost Institute For FamilyLiving, Inc.

The advice in this book can be a valuable
addition to the advice of your family health
care specialists and is designed for your use
under their care and direction

Copyright 2002 by The Philip Lief Group, Inc.
All rights reserved

2002 Revision of First Printing (1988) Produced by The
Van Ost Institute For Family Living, Inc.
150 East Palisade Ave, Englewood, NJ 07631

2002 Book Design by Connie Parker, Parker Design Group

Printed by: Boyd Printing Company, Inc., Albany, NY

Library of Congress Cataloging-in-Publication Data
(For 1st Printing: September 1988):

Van Ost, William C.
   Warning signs: a parent's guide to in-time intervention in drug
and alcohol abuse / William C. Van Ost and Elaine Van Ost.
   p. cm.
   Includes index.
   1. Children - United States - Drug Use. 2. Teenagers -
United States - Drug Use. 3. Drug abuse - United States -
Prevention. 4. Narcotic addicts - United States - Family
Relationships. 5. Alcoholics - United States - Family
relationships.   I. Van Ost, Elaine.   II. Title.
HV5824.C45V35   1988
362.2'9 - dc19
ISBN 0-446-38727-4 (pbk.) (U.S.A.) /   88-5773
0-446-38728-2 (pbk.) (Canada)   CIP

CONTENTS

ACKNOWLEDGEMENTS

We want to thank the many people who have given us their encouragement, knowledge,and love.Those people who, by either personal involvement with us,or through their own books, lectures, films, articles and tapes have shared their experience, strength, and hope. For the pioneers in this field of addictive illnesses, to our close friends and co-workers, we say "thank you" to you all.

A special note of appreciation to our mentors, particularly to Ruth Maxwell whose teachings set a new course for our lives; to The Rt. Rev. Jack McKelvey who helped the Van Ost Institute For Family Living find its first home and become a reality; to "Mac" Macdonald for his advice and for his willingness to write the Introduction to this book; to our special friends and confidants: Mel Sandler, Vicki Gannon and Jeanne Rigaud; to Bill and Lois Wilson, and to the many others who have touched and affected our lives and, who we may have inadvertently failed to mention.

This book is a compendium of years of our own experiential learning, plus the knowledge we absorbed from the literature provided by those who who have preceded us: Rockelle Lerner, Earnie Larsen, Fr. Joseph C. Martin, Celia Delfano, Tom Perrin, Scott Peck. Virginia Satir, Judy Siexas, Timmen Cermak, Charles Deutch, Oakly Ray, Phil Oliver-Diaz, Dr. Joe Cruse, Sharon Wegscheider-Cruse, Claudia Black, Vernon Johnson, and the late Janet Woititz.

Thanks go to those members of the American Academy of Pediatrics who encouraged us in our successful efforts to convince the Academy's leadership of the urgent need to form a Committee on Substance Abuse. Now in place for over twenty years, the Committee is expanding what had been, for most pediatricians, a scant knowledge base, resulting in what was a sad lack of concern with the prevention, the early recognition, or the management of substance abuse by our nation's young. For their efforts, we offer special kudos to: Drs. Stan Karp, Joe Bogdan, Art Maron, Tony DeSpirito, George Comerci, Sue Aronson, Joe Sanders, Richard Heyman, Peter Rodgers and to the many others who saw the need and cared enough to do something about it.

We would be remiss if we didn't also acknowledge the work of others who made our book possible: For the first edition: the late Jamie Rothstein, of Warner Books, Editor; Kevin Osborn of The Philip Lief Group, Inc, Producer; and Peg Parkinson. For this edition, which we hope to provide at little or no cost to as many young parents as possible, we offer thanks on their behalf to Don Schaefer of The Palisades Educational Trust which is providing major funding for this project; to Steve and the late Al Riecker for all their encouragement and, particularly, for finding a printer willing to tackle this project: the Boyd Printing Company of Albany, NY. Further financial support has been made available through the generosity of the Lillian Pitkin Schenck Fund, The Van Pelt Foundation, The Community Chest of Leonia, NJ, Inc, The Bergen County (NJ) Board of Chosen Freeholders and to the many other supporters of our non-profit addiction treatment center: The Van Ost Institute for Family Living.

We shall be forever grateful to the Institute's Board of Trustees, past and present, for the vital "pediatric" role that its members assumed from its founding and throughout its childhood. During its adolescence (as it is for a teenager, a difficult time), certain trustees worked particularly hard to assure the Institute's survival. For those untiring efforts we owe a special thanks to Glenn Johnson, Florie Meltzer, Judy and Harlan Bliss, Ferris Saydah, Bob Ricca, Richard Gregg , Bob Cooper, and to our dear friend, Lou Weisblatt. The Institute, now safely into adulthood, continues to grow, thanks to the dedication of our other Trustees: Pastor Keith Attles, Dr. Michelle DeAntonio,Ron Bell, Larry Feld, John Johl, Gloria Layne, Celeste Oranchak, Doug Seiferling and Honorary Trustees from both political parties: U.S. Sen. Bob Torricelli, U.S. Reps. Marge Roukema and Steve Rothman, and former Freeholder Chmn. Jimmy Sheehan.

To the Van Ost Institute's volunteers and staff, particularly to Bill Carlos, Jr., its present Executive Director and contributor to this edition of our book; to Bill's wife, Jacki Carlos; and to Bobby White, the Institute's Office Manager, Secretary, and Master of all Trades, we offer special thanks for supporting our hopes and dreams of providing help to families affected by addiction.

INTRODUCTION

This book by two recognized experts in the field of drug abuse diagnosis, treatment, and rehabilitation is a book about more than just drugs. It is a book about the family and how it functions.

Elaine and William C. Van Ost, M.D., describe in commonsense terms how and why kids get hooked on drugs—including alcohol, the drug most frequently abused. They describe how and why parents contribute to the problem, or at least enable it to worsen.

I am betting that you will find yourself somewhere in this book: probably in more than one place. The Van Osts describe scores of scenarios that happen every day in families everywhere in this country. What you may learn as you find yourself, your kids, and your friends in this book is that scenarios you have experienced or

witnessed as problems had at their core drug abuse—
and you never realized it until now!

The disease of drug addiction is clearly a problem
that has been with us for as long as anyone can
remember. What is new is that it has been affecting
younger and younger kids, and that the variety of drugs
of abuse is spreading without regard to social standing,
education, or any other supposed indicators of success.
Unfortunately, drug abuse in this country no longer just
happens to the other guy—it is endemic.

At the center of this scary—sometimes gruesome—
change is the family. By using a variety of examples, the
authors deftly show how parents have often failed to see
or to confront a problem. In our world of constantly
increasing pressures, single-parent families, and families with two working parents, this is hardly surprising.
In a world where kids are increasingly seduced at ever-
earlier ages to try drugs, sex, and other secrets of the
adult world, it is not surprising that parents as well as
kids are finding it increasingly difficult to "Just Say No."

Through this pall of gloom the Van Osts have cut a
refreshing beam of light. They lay out in this book no-
nonsense recipes for tackling the problem of drug abuse
in kids—ideally, before recovery becomes a long shot. In
the process, they rediscover for the reader a bit of
wisdom many of us heard from our parents and grandparents: Kids need, and often want, a protective environment.

Just as important, the authors provide—again, in
practical detail—a recipe for heading off the unfortunate
end for many a young abuser: suicide. The successful
approach employed by many throughout the country—
including the authors themselves, at their Van Ost
Institute for Family Living—is tried and true. That

twelve-step approach to self-help, as employed by Alcoholics Anonymous, Al-Anon, Alateen, Narcotics Anonymous, and Adult Children of Alcoholics, is described by the authors in a way that provides many of the answers to the questions of an agonized parent.

This book is a must for any parent struggling with a problem with his or her adolescent, or even preadolescent; it is a must for anyone who knows of such a problem and cares enough to do something about it.

DONALD IAN MACDONALD, M.D., F.A.A.P.

*Director, White House Drug Abuse
Policy Office; and Special Assistant to
the President and Administrator, Alcohol, Drug, Mental
Health Administration.*

PROLOGUE

We both got the idea of founding the Van Ost Institute For Family Living at the same moment in mid-summer, 1983. We were standing on a Connecticut beach, watching the sun go down. Everybody else had gone home. Then suddenly, the figure of a young girl, 12 or 13 at most, we guessed, emerged from a nearby boathouse. Staggering a little, she was holding the inside of her left elbow with the fingers of her right hand: the classic shooting-up gesture. She turned and walked unsteadily away from us toward town.

We were still there, rooted by the tragedy of what we'd just seen when a man, walking his dog along the beach, came our way. We told him about the girl in the boathouse. He just shrugged. "It's the summer people," he said. "There's nothing anybody can do about it."

Right there, right then, we made up our minds that there *was* something that could be done about it, and we've been doing it ever since.

Our Institute is not a fix-it shop where you can drop off a troubled youngster for a tune-up or a tire patch. But there are any number of ways we help families in trouble, and this book is written in the belief that we can tell you what you should know and what you should do about a child of your own who may now----or someday---be giving you some sleepless nights

Our goal is to make family life better for everyone concerned. We want you, as parents, to know what you need to know to deal with problems of chemical dependency. . . . and how to spot warning signs of trouble ahead. The sooner you pick up signals, the better for everyone. We ourselves are parents, of five adult children, and we know what growing up in dysfunctional families can be like: awful. We're on your side in what can be a tough battle, a battle to save young lives-----and to keep your own sanity. We want you, as mothers and fathers, to understand the way you behave as parents, which can be vital to the understanding of your kids.

As you read this book, please remember that whenever we use the terms alcoholic/drinking or drug abuse or drugging to describe a chemical substance abuse, we do not, in most cases, mean just one *or* the other. Since alcohol is in itself a drug , all terms are interchangeable. Use the one that applies to you.

Our own term for addiction----to drugs of any sort---- is "the mushroom syndrome." Left in the dark, cultivated mushrooms thrive, but when they are exposed to light and air, they stop growing. We want this book to shed the light of understanding about drugs in households all over America.

Helping families get better is *our* addiction

Dr. Bill and Elaine Van Ost
September 1988

Addendum:

Since the initial printing of this book in 1988, much has changed in the field of addiction; in both the basic understanding of the neurophysiology involved and in appropriate application of this knowledge by treatment providers .

New light shed on the activity of certain brain centers as they respond to addictive stimuli, and the recognition that addicted individuals have certain genetic markers in common, points even more clearly to confirming our view that addiction is an *intergeneration disease.*

As a result of managed care practices, the numbers of denials for in-patient care, particularly for children, has increased so markedly that financial concerns have become a major factor in clinical decision-making. To meet that challenge, our Institute has developed intensive family-oriented outpatient treatment programs which are producing satisfying results and have, by necessity, become the norm.

The problem of nicotine addiction, to our regret, was unaddressed in our 1988 edition, but is now widely recognised as far more addictive than alcohol, and like alcohol, is a major "gateway" drugs on the road to the use of illicit addictive chemicals by our nation's children.

Dr. Bill and Elaine
May 2002

1

IT COULD HAPPEN
TO ANY KID

SOME COLD HARD FACTS

BACK WHEN IT
ALL BEGAN

For the very young among us, Woodstock may be nothing more than ancient history, relegated to a dim past that perhaps includes vague perceptions of the wartime Forties, the wimpy Fifties, and the spacey Sixties. For those of us who may ourselves have been flower children, the Woodstock era represents a high-water mark of the past. It held the bright promise of a future shaped by a belief in what was called "the greening of America," a country to be reborn in the hippie counterculture.

For those reflecting today on the stoned society of the Eighties, the Woodstock decade is what many consider to be the one that turned respectable American on to drugs. Before the Sixties, drug abuse was a problem most often linked to poverty, or to the rarefied lives of jazz musicians.

In the Seventies, another pattern of use became plain: Drugs were recreational. The Vietnam war ended, but its own drug story continued. The counterculture was assimilated into the mainstream of American life, and usage spread. College students and young career people alike made pot almost as acceptable as tobacco, and cocaine was glamorized as the life of the party. If drugs caused problems, it was always for somebody else—somebody in glittery Hollywood or jet-set New York City who made too much of a good thing.

The message today, as we head for the Nineties, is that this country is caught up in an acknowledged epidemic of drug and alcohol abuse (alcohol being, of course, a drug in liquid form). The bad news is not just that drugs are now accessible in every part of the country—not even rural America is immune—but that the drugs themselves aren't what they used to be: Almost everything sold today is far more potent than its "benign" antecedent. A former official of the Federal Drug Enforcement Agency likens the difference to that between buying a bicycle and a Sherman tank.

Perhaps the saddest fact we must face today, however, is that the drug epidemic no longer threatens only those who are old enough to know better. Each year, the age of initiation, which was once mid- or late adolescence, takes an alarming drop. A 1987 government survey found that 30% of our ten-year-olds feel peer pressure to drink.

SOME FIGURES THAT DON'T LIE

The United States Department of Health and Human Resources, launching another round of its war on drugs in 1987, aimed its "Be Smart—Don't Start" campaign—which included a music video and TV and radio public-service announcements—at eight- to 12-year-olds. Print material, directed to teachers, physicians, parents, and community leaders, acknowledged that "alcohol is the most readily available and most frequently used drug among young people today," and supplied the following figures about school-age kids:

- 91% of high-school seniors have tried alcohol.
- 65% of high-school seniors are current drinkers (meaning, they've consumed alcohol one or more times within the previous month).
- 39% of high-school seniors are involved in heavy-party drinking (five or more drinks in a row) at least once or twice every weekend.
- 45% of high-school seniors think their friends approve of this behavior.
- 39% of high-school seniors believe there is a great risk associated with heavy-party drinking, as compared with 71% who believe that there is a great risk associated with regular marijuana use.
- 5% of high-school seniors drink daily or nearly daily.
- 55% of high-school seniors first used alcohol in the ninth grade; 22% in or before seventh or eighth grade; and 8% in or before sixth grade.

- 12.3 years is the average age for first alcohol use.
- 30% of 13-year-old boys and 22% of 13-year-old girls are current drinkers.
- More male adolescents drink than females; the number of female drinkers, however, is increasing more rapidly than the number of male drinkers.
- The largest increase in drinking occurs between the sixth and seventh grades—it goes from 10% to 22%.

WHY ALCOHOL?

"Thank God it's not drugs," is too often what parents say when they learn that their youngsters have been drinking. In fact, alcohol is a "gateway" drug that can be lethal on its own.

The earlier a youngster drinks, the more likely he or she is to drink more frequently later on—and to combine alcohol with marijuana. A national survey recently reported that about half the students who were moderate to heavy drinkers said they also smoked pot, as compared to only a tenth of those who were abstainers or light drinkers.

Kids choose alcohol because it's easier to come by than illicit drugs (never mind that it's illegal for them to drink at all). And the simplest place to get it is at home, where its presence conveys an implied sanction of its use. But kids in high school—and now, those in secondary school as well—don't drink in a social context. They drink, more often than not, to get drunk.

There are many parents who believe that it's okay for teenagers to drink "in moderation," and reason that in fact it's not a bad idea to teach their children to drink at home because such "lessons" will keep them from getting into trouble elsewhere. These people, we believe, are entirely misguided. Their attitude reflects a society that says it's okay to drink, but not to be a drunk; it's okay to be a party-goer, but not okay to throw up in somebody else's bathroom; it's okay to provide cocaine for your guests, but not okay to run out of money because you yourself are hooked on it.

These are usually the same people who think they have to accept the idea that kids are going to go ahead and drink no matter what—and that there's nothing-we-can-do-about-it.

In most states serving alcohol to minors is against the law. Parents who condone teenage drinking are parents who don't know about, or don't want to see, the truly frightening harm that can come from mixing alcohol and adolescence. The same parents who know that the high-school football coach forbids his players to drink while in training are affirming what they already know and accept—that the team may drink at other times, however illegally. They are often the ones who believe not only in "safe" drinking at home but support "safe ride" programs for teens who've been drinking. *Of course* no one wants automobile accidents, but that's not the point. The point is that in creating such a safety program parents give their kids the message: "We know you're going to drink at parties, so to keep you out of trouble on the highways we'll cover for you when you disregard the law." We say the law is the law, and you as responsible adults are obliged to respect the law and teach your children to do the same. Your child's *life* is at stake.

And the laws are there for good reasons. When teenagers add alcohol to their inexperience behind the wheel, they're soliciting disaster. Each year, nearly 230,000 youngsters are injured or maimed as a result of drinking-and-driving; 8,000 of them die.

JUST A SWALLOW AWAY

It isn't necessarily a swallow—it could just as well be a toke, or a snort. It often begins with tobacco: Nicotine is one of the most addictive chemicals known, and smoking is one of the hardest habits to break. For every group of four kids who try tobacco, one will still be trying to quit twenty years later. (Even Russian roulette, at five-to-one, beats those odds.) Moreover, tobacco is unique among drugs in that people often smoke a cigarette to keep alert and deal with a problem that's coming their way and then light another once they've dealt with the problem and feel they deserve to relax.

Over 80% of teenage cigarette smokers also try marijuana. And over 60% of pot smokers go on to use other illicit drugs. Diet pills and "study aids," particularly among girls, also have gateway drug roles that can lead them down the path to drug dependency.

Marianne G. had just turned 19 when we saw her in August of 1987. She'd grown up in Connecticut with an alcoholic father and a high-strung mother who was so enmeshed in her husband's drinking problem that, as Marianne told us, "She never even noticed anything I did. I smoked pot when I was ten, and it was 'ludes and coke by the tenth grade, when I dropped out. I came home really high one night and I didn't have any more money and they weren't there yet so I took everything I could find, including a really good radio. And I just left and they never knew."

Marianne wandered around the country, using "a lot of acid." In California she found a boyfriend who gave her IV heroin for her birthday.

How did she support her new habit?

"Guys always tried to buy you for sex and stuff, so what I would do is get high with them and tell them I'd meet them somewhere, and I'd take off. . . . Maybe with the next guy I'd do the same thing. A lot of times, though, I did have sex because I needed to get more stuff."

Over the years, Marianne had five abortions. Periodically she would return home when she ran out of money. One of those times, her family sent her to a rehabilitation center in Michigan, where she stayed for two months. She went back on drugs within two days of being discharged. Today she's in a halfway house we found for her after she'd gone through yet another rehab program of several weeks.

It was her mother who brought her to us—Marianne had found her way back to Connecticut, once again. Her father was still drinking. "That upset me a lot," Marianne told us, "but I was boozing too, so that doesn't mean much, does it?"

Marianne gave us every assurance that "I really want to go straight this time," but there was no way we could be reassuring to her mother. From our experience with kids this far down the line, we can't give her much more than a 25% chance of recovery.

2

IT COULD HAPPEN
TO *YOUR* KID

UNDERSTANDING WHY KIDS TAKE DRUGS

AN ESCAPE FROM
GROWING PAINS

Adolescence, as we all can recall, is a tough enough time without complications. Plagued by everything from acne to being turned down for dates, from changing voices to uncertainty about careers, teenagers agonize equally over momentary setbacks ("Why didn't he/she say hello to me?") and lifetime decisions ("Should I be a CPA or go to law school?"). Looking for identities of their own, they turn to others to bolster their shaky self-esteem, in a desperate need to belong. And each generation looks for risks and thrills—and makes a point of tuning out parental advice.

A certain amount of rebellion is normal: Unheeding

the warnings of their elders, youngsters want to look for their own answers. To reach emotional, physical, and sexual maturity, adolescents *must* develop individuality and autonomy, separating themselves gradually, pulling away from home while they establish adult value systems and form commitments outside the family. These processes often involve a lot of emotional pain; learning to handle it is part of maturing.

Drug use interferes with this progession of growth. If a teenager feels alienated from others, whether parents or pals, and turns to chemicals as a way to ease his or her difficulties, then "rebellion" is not a way of reaching adulthood but a sidetrack that can lead to further, and prolonged, immaturity.

The Kids Most Likely . . .

The kids most likely to get into trouble with drugs are the ones who aren't comfortable about being themselves; who feel like outsiders; who can't seem to tell the difference between what they need and what they'd like to have; who want instant gratification; who don't listen; who don't accept responsibility for what happens to them because they can't accept the fact that their behavior has consequences. (You've surely heard, in one variation or another, "I didn't get a good grade in that class because the teacher has it in for me," which really means: He didn't get a good grade because he hasn't bothered to study. Or, "I got dropped as a cheerleader because the others don't think I'm cute enough," which really means: She got dropped because she missed two practice sessions in a row.)

What makes children susceptible to drugs is the fact that they are still, after all, children. Because they aren't old enough to have developed coping mechanisms—ways of encountering problems and working them through to solutions that make them more prepared to meet the disappointments, the emotional upsets, the *Sturm und Drang* that life will hand them as they mature—they may come to think that drugs solve their problems by changing their mood. Getting hooked, of course, creates a whole different set of problems—and a child waylaid on the progress to adulthood is in danger of remaining a child forever. Acting like a teenager at 14 is one thing; at 28, it can be tragic.

Chemical dependency refers to any process of chemical use over which we have no control once we've started. It keeps us unaware of what's going on inside us: We don't have to deal with pain or problems because we suppress the feelings they give us. What kids don't realize is that eventually, if we go on using something to protect us from the bad things like anger or depression or fear, we are not going to be able to feel the good things, either—elation or pride or joy or love.

NO ONE EVER TOLD THEM DRUGS WERE GOOD FOR THEM, SO WHY DO THEY EXPERIMENT?

Peer pressure. Most kids try drugs for the same reasons they adopt weird haircuts and outlandish clothes and talk in a slang code that's all their own—because it makes them feel like part of the crowd, and because their friends invite them to come on and do what the really "in" kids are doing.

Peer pressure is inevitable and seductive; the need

to belong is vital. Adolescents can't tell everything to their parents; they need secrets, they need space. But the danger of peer group influence is that, where drugs are concerned for example, vulnerable kids go from seeing one or two friends do it to a conviction that "everybody does it." And peer groups often inspire great loyalty. Even when they know about someone's heavy drug use, youngsters are careful not to spill the beans for fear of having others think of them as finks, or narcs.

Going along for the ride. For teenagers risk-taking is important. They go against the grain of adult opinion in seeking adventure, and find that drugs offer an enjoyable high for little or no effort on their part. ("Who, *me* get in trouble? No way—I can handle it.") The only danger they perceive is that of being caught—by parents, teachers, or the cops. According to one national survey, 42% of high-school seniors saw "no harm" in having five or more drinks every weekend.

The rock scene. It's permeated by the values and practices of the drug culture. Rock stars become cult heroes; many of them do drugs and their young followers know it—and identify with their lifestyles.

Rock concerts can create their own problems. They are often held at tax-supported sports stadiums, civic centers, and public concert halls. At concerts in many cities, drugs are openly sold and used. Rest rooms are crowded with kids throwing up from combinations of what they've been taking. Most parents don't know this; they drop children off and pick them up later, or they assign teenagers to drive the ten- and 12-year-olds home. (What parents also may not realize is that many public officials have given up on enforcing drug laws and tend to shift the blame for youthful drug-taking onto ineffectual parenting.)

The media influence. Drug-culture values have long existed on TV, shown up in photojournalism, and been made obvious with videocassettes. An unending barrage of commericals glamorizes the lives led by beer and wine drinkers.

Head shops. The practice of locating them near junior high and high schools, or near snack and record stores where kids hang out, is a tip-off to the paraphernalia business's regard for children as a major growth market. Impressionable secondary-school children can buy drug-related toys, games, comic books. Though most patrons of these shops are adults, the commercial message to gullible kids is, "Drugs are fun!"

THE TRUTH—AND CONSEQUENCES—OF USING CHEMICALS

We all know that drugs do far more than merely alter mood. Here are just some of the physical effects caused by the most popular ones in use today. Bear in mind that several of them are far more potent than they were some years ago. Today's marijuana, for instance, is ten times as potent as it was in the sixties. Cocaine, too: The purity of today's street supply is three times that of only a decade ago—and the price has gone down.

Alcohol

The most commonly used drug by children today, is often the most overlooked drug as well. Studies have shown that after using this "gateway drug" to first experience intoxication, kids are more likely to try other drugs while drinking. In potency and effect: 1 ounce distilled spirits = 1 twelve ounce can of beer = 1 five ounce glass of wine.

Drug Dependency can lead to:
- Birth defects
- Damage to liver, heart and pancreas
- Malnutrition
- High blood pressure
- Neurological damage to the brain
- Hormonal imbalance, keeping the body in a permanent state of stress

Look for:
- Hidden bottles in unlikely places such as cereal boxes, inside of toilet tanks, rolled up in rugs, stashed in boots, stuffed in crevices in the attic or garage
- A collection of empty bottles of extracts such as vanilla or rum, as they often have high levels of alcohol in them
- The scent of alcohol in open soda cans, tea cups or glasses from which your child is drinking or are laying about in your child's bedroom
- Noticeably lower levels in bottles kept around the house

Marijuana ("Grass," "Pot," "Weed")

This crude drug derived from the plant Cannabis Sativa is ten times greater in strength than the marijuana of the 1970's. The mindaltering (psychoactive) ingredient of marijuana is THC (delta-9-tetrahydrocannabinol) but more than 400 other chemicals are in the plant. The drug's potency depends on several factors: the amount of THC used, the time of year harvested, the weather, the soil, etc. A marijuana "joint" or cigarette is made from dried particles of the plant (leaves, seeds and stems).

Hashish ("Hash") is produced by pressing the leaves and the flowers of the marijuana plant into cakes or slabs of resin which have the color of tar, licorice or mustard-colored taffy. It is much stronger than the crude plant, containing five to ten times the amount of THC. Hash oil, the brownish pressings of the plant, may contain up to fifty percent THC and can be injected into ordinary tobacco cigarettes for concealment of usage.

Drug Dependency Can Lead To:

- Lung damage similar to that caused by cigarettes, resulting in later cancer
- Birth defects
- Weakened immune system
- Impairment of psychomotor functions
- Impairment of learning ability and short-term memory

Look for:

- Oregano-like material with an odor suggestive of burnt rope or hemp, which may be kept ("stashed") in small plastic bags or brown envelopes

• "Joints," which look like skinny, hand-rolled cigarettes
• Pipes with small metal screens in the bowls, or "bongs" (water pipes)
• Matchbook-sized cigarette rolling papers (thin small white sheets with the consistency of tissue paper, that can be picked up at many newsstands, supermarkets and drug stores)
• "Roach clips"--dental bib clips, or feather earrings with clips which are used to hold "joint" butts ("roaches")
• Chiclet-size or smaller pellets of hashish, and tiny metal pipes, small enough to hide in a cigarette pack.

Cocaine ("Coke")

Many adolescents view using this drug as a rite of passage and a symbol of affluence, making this a very "trendy" drug. Native to South America, and derived from the cocoa bush, its leaves are harvested and soaked in a mixture of chemicals until it is broken down into the cocaine salt. This salt is dried and crushed into a snowy, white, bitter-tasting powder which can be injected, smoked or snorted. Heavy users will attempt to offset the "low" period or "crash" following the drug-produced "high" by seeking more cocaine or by using other drugs such as alcohol, valium or marijuana to ease the symptoms.

Drug Dependency Can Lead To:

• Strokes and epileptic seizures (cocaine acts directly on the heart and the area of the brain that controls the heart and lungs)
• Nausea, vomiting and sore throat
• Fatigue, yet insomnia

- Nosebleeds, nasal ulcers and eventual loss of the skin and cartilage that separates nostrils
- Sinus problems
- Mood swings, including depression and paranoia
- An inevitable and severe "crash" when the effects of the drug wear off

Look For:

- White powder in glassine or plastic envelopes, or small plastic vials
- Such paraphernalia as single-edged razor blades, diagonally cut straws or tightly-rolled paper, mirrors, miniature spoons on jewelry chains or key chains.
- An inappropriately long "pinky" fingernail on your child's hand

Crack ("Rock")

Crack is powdered cocaine mixed with baking soda and water to form a paste which hardens, looking like off-white rock salt. When smoked ("freebased"), there is an audible crackling sound, giving the drug its name. This drug is cheaper than powdered cocaine, and also more appealing to some because usage can be less conspicuous than snorting, and because it produces a more immediate and more intense euphoria. It is most commonly sold in small vials or in folded paper or foil. Instant addiction has been reported but, more likely, it takes from a week to several weeks. Nobody is certain.

Drug Dependency Can Lead To:

- Rapid heartbeat and increased blood pressure
- Heart and lung problems
- Seizures
- Death

Look For:

- Thumbnail size vials with colorful tops in which the crack may be packaged
- A small metal pipe—the same kind as used for hashish

PCP ("Angel Dust")

PCP (Phenylcyclidine) was first developed in the 1950's as an anesthetic, but because of its tendency to cause hallucinations, was taken off the market. The chemical is now classified as a hallucinogen or psychedelic because it can affect a person's perceptions, sensations, thinking, self-awareness and emotions. Although illegal, it is easily manufactured and is often sold as mescaline, THC, or a number of other drugs that can take many forms: tablets, capsules, or a crystal-like powder. It can be swallowed, smoked, sniffed or injected. Cigarettes made of tobacco, parsley or marijuana can be "spiked" by PCP before smoked.

Drug Dependency Can Lead To:

- Permanent impairment of brain function: motor control, memory, and concentration
- The inducement of a psychotic state, delusions, hallucinations, and violent behavior
- The occurrence of frequent accidents and injuries
- The inducement of a catatonic state: mute staring into space, unable to communicate

Look For:

- Since it takes so many forms, there is *no* way to identify it

LSD ("Acid")

Discovered in 1938, LSD is one of the most potent mood-changing chemicals whose effects are unpredictable. Manufactured from an ingredient in ergot, a fungus that grows on rye and other grains, LSD is an odorless, colorless and tasteless material, which is sold on the street in the form of tablets, capsules or occasionally a liquid. It is usually taken orally and is often added to absorbent paper and divided in squares with each square, representing one dose. A similar technique is used to hide the drug in small pellets that look like candy.

Drug Dependency Can Lead To:

• Impairment of judgment, and an altered perception of time and space
• Sensory distortions of vision
• An emotional imbalance and dreamlike states while awake
• Probable permanent damage to some brain systems

Look For:

• Sheets of paper with stained dots ("blotter acid") or thin squares of gelatin that look like glass ("window panes") in plastic envelopes

Amphetamines ("Speed," "Bennys," "Crystal")

This class of drug was first synthesized in the 1930's, quickly finding a variety of medical uses as a stimulant, appetite supressor and for certain attention disorders found in children. It's "alerting" qualities were noted early on by students cramming for exams and truck drivers who didn't want to fall asleep at the wheel. Amphetamines appear in many forms such as capsules and tablets, produced by both legal and illicit means.

Drug Dependency Can Lead To:

• Insomnia
• Loss of appetite
• Heart attack and stroke
• The destruction of nerve cells in the brain
• A condition similar to paranoid schizophrenia
• Experiencing a severe "crash" when drug's effects wear off

Look For:

• *Any* pills found with a child's belongings

Heroin ("Junk," "Smack")

This drug accounts for ninety percent of the opiate abuse in the United States. Opiates, which also include morphine and codeine often referred to as narcotics, are a group of drugs used medically to relieve pain but which also have a high potential for addiction. Heroin can be a white or brownish powder which is usually diluted or "cut" with other substances such as milk sugar or quinine. Heroin can be a white or brownish powder which is usually dissolved in water and then injected. Most street preparations of heroin are diluted Opiates and come in a variety of forms including capsules, tablets, syrups, solutions and suppositories.

Drug Dependency Can Lead To:

• Increased risk of infection such as AIDS, and hepatitis
• Skin abcesses
• Inflammation of the heart from contaminated needles
• A depression of the central nervous system, resulting in respiratory failure, convulsions, coma and death

Look For:

• White powder resembling baking soda, in glassine or plastic envelopes
• Diabetic or other syringes
• Bottle caps or spoons with burns on them

Barbiturates
("Barbs," "Downers") And Other Sedatives

Barbiturates, as a group, form one major category of sedative-hypnotics. Often referred to as sleeping pills, they are used to treat anxiety and to promote sleep, among other things. Some well-known barbiturates are secobarbitol (Seconal) and phenobarbital (Nembutal). The other major category of sedative-hypnotics are the benzodiazepines or tranquilizers such as diazepam (Valium) and clordiazepoxide (Librium). A few sedative-hypnotics do not fit either categories. These include methaqualone (Quaaludes), ethchlorvynol (Placidyl), and meprobamate (Miltown). All of these drugs are dangerous and can kill if improperly used, particularly when taken with the drug, alcohol. All are sold on the street in a variety of forms of capsules, tablets and pills. "Look alikes" manufactured to look like sedative hypnotics and mimic their effects are often sold on the street to kids as the real thing. These often contain over-the-counter drugs such as antihistamines and decongestants and tend to cause drowsiness. Taken with other drugs like alcohol, these also can be highly dangerous.

Drug Dependency Can Lead To:

• Liver damage
• Anemia
• Respiratory failure, coma and/or death caused by an overdose
• Convulsions caused by sudden withdrawal

Look For:

• *Any* capsules, tablets and pills, loose or in vials

Taking drugs in combination has also become popular. Not long ago, mixing cocaine with other drugs was uncommon; today, it's more of a rule than an exception. The effects of this mixing are unpredictable; street drugs are hardly quality controlled. Many of the substances work together synergistically, each magnifying the effects of the other—which increases the likelihood of severe and even fatal consequences.

3

DOES THE APPLE FALL

FAR FROM THE TREE?

FAMILY DYNAMICS 101

Mike R., 16, was referred to us by his parents, who hadn't even suspected his drinking problem until he wrecked the family car for the third time. After hearing his inventive excuses following the first two accidents, they obligingly had the car repaired—and handed him back the keys.

To say that parents tend to be naive about their own children is to put it mildly. An Emory University study of six hundred high-school students in Atlanta revealed that a third of their parents thought their kids had used alcohol within the previous month. In fact, *more than two-thirds* of the students themselves reported that indeed they *had* been drinking at that time.

Judy C., a persistent user of pot at 13, found herself

pregnant at that age. She had accepted the boy's sexual advances, she said, when "we were both stoned."

There are still things we don't know about the disease of addiction, both to alcohol and to other drugs—remember, they're interchangeable—but what we do know is that the kids who are most at risk of developing drug problems come from family backgrounds of two extremes: those in which there is heavy drinking, and those in which there's no drinking at all.

Good—since you drink moderately, that lets your kid off the hook, doesn't it? No. Because there isn't a kid anywhere who's invulnerable to the drug epidemic.

It doesn't matter where you live or whether or not you went to college or whether you're black or white or rich or poor or happily married or unhappily divorced. Nor does it matter where your child goes to school or what kind of a youngster he or she is—sunny or somber, popular or not, at the top of the class or flunking out.

Your kid is just as likely to try drugs as any other kid—and that's *very* likely.

THE OSTRICH EFFECT

Keeping your head in a hole in the ground doesn't help you any more than it does an ostrich—pretty soon, whatever it is you don't want to see is probably going to make itself all the more forcibly felt. So please, look around you—not just at your community, or at the schools, or at the courts, but at the scene you know best: the one in your own household. What's the message you're giving your kids?

Think first about your own drinking or drugging habits and what, as parents, you may be teaching by example.

- Do you urge drinks on guests?
- Do you regard mild drunkenness as amusing?
- Do you sometimes say you "need" a drink?
- Do you pretend you just don't see your spouse's drinking or drugging?
- Do you regard your spouse's drinking or drugging with irritation, or terror, or martyrdom?
- Do you turn the other way or think it's funny when your kid grows marijuana at home? Or when he or she wears drug-culture T-shirts?

WHAT DO WE HAVE IN COMMON?

A family is, in one simple sense, a social system: It is made up of individuals who are bound together by ties of love and dependence as well as by physical and emotional needs. But though all families have dozens of things in common, each one is genetically unique. We urge you to look hard at your own, because there are important inferences you can draw from knowing as much as possible about generations and branches of your family that are distant from you and your children.

Your Family Genogram: A Diagnostic Tool You Can Use

The genogram, or family tree, is an important part of every assessment and diagnosis we do at the Van Ost Institute.

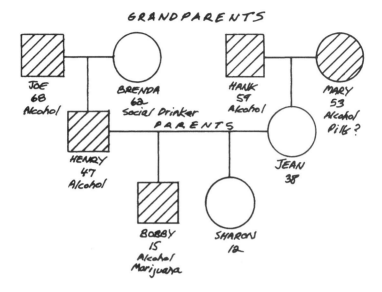

Since a major indicator of possible chemical dependency is a history of use in the family, what we do at the institute is fill in an outline similar to the one below, at each interview using information from the patient and family members. The genogram then becomes part of the entire picture of diagnosis, along with questions about the physical, mental, and emotional health of everyone involved.

In addition to the simplified sample genogram below, we have provided you with an open outline which you may complete for yourself, (Appendix 1). Other family members may want to try filling one out too, so make plenty of copies.

The sample depicts a family in which the father, Henry, age 47, and the mother, Jean, age 38, have two children, Bobby, age 15, and Sharon, age 12. The grandparents on each side of the family complete the basic family picture.

The genogram can be continued on each side of the family to include great-grandparents, although it's often difficult to obtain clear information regarding drinking and drug use for any ancestors beyond grandparents. Chemical depending was even a better-kept family secret further back in time than it is now.

"Hatch" marks across the squares of grandparent Joe, father Henry, and young Bobby indicate drinking problems or alcoholism. Notice how, in this case, the alcoholism is passed on from father to son to grandson—a common pattern. On the other side of the family, Jean's father is alcoholic and there is some question about Jean's mother's drinking and pill use (indicated by light hatching and a question mark). Again, note that daughters of alcoholics will frequently marry alcholics or men prone to addiction.

A genogram can be extended to include not only great-grandparents, but aunts, uncles, second wives or husbands, and other family additions as well. Just name them so you will know who they are when you are finished.

Some important questions to ask yourself, or others, as you fill out your own genogram:

1. Whose drinking *bothered* me?

You may not be sure whether a family member is alcoholic or drug-addicted, but if you ask yourself whether it *bothered* or *concerned* you, it can often allow you to see certain behaviors that you might deny or gloss over or make excuses for if you had to decide whether to apply a definite label of alcoholic or drug addict to someone.

Other questions to help you uncover addiction:

2. Did his or her mood change when drinking?
3. Does a person use pills often for headaches? Diets? Nerves?
4. If unable to find or get the needed pills, is or was there irritability?
5. Is he or she an embarrassment at parties?
6. Is there anger about a person's drinking or drug use (on the part of those close to the person?)
7. Is it understood that someone's drinking or drug use is not to be discussed?
8. Did or does a relative or child seem never to have enough money?
9. Did or does he or she not quite "make the grade," always with excuses from close family members?
10. Does everyone prepare for Uncle Louie or Aunt Tillie's wild behavior at family weddings?
11. How does Uncle Louie's wife feel about his "craziness"?
12. Does marrying alcoholics or addicts seem almost normal in your family?

These, plus any other questions you may have of your own, will help you complete your genogram.

After you have completed the genogram to the best of your ability, ask other family members to add their opinions or feelings. If you encounter reluctance to talk about it, or teasing, or any expressions of anger, or resistance, there could well be a problem. If there are widely varying opinions from family members about who drank and who didn't, or if there are strong statements of denial or embarrassment, there is the need to look further.

Use this family genogram to help you know your family better. The awareness that results may bring you closer to professional help and recovery. Whatever you do, don't ignore it. It's too important.

FAMILY INTERACTION

The sense of connectedness in a family can serve it either well or badly: The family unit is rather like a mobile— each part of the whole is affected by the movements of the others. The success of a family as a social system depends on the balance it achieves by meeting the different wants, and accepting the different contributions, of its members.

Those families that function well allow members to maintain their own identities while also giving themselves to others. The roles of givers and takers change, of course, in different situations as well as at different stages of life and growth. Healthy families can take change in stride, accommodating one another as needed to provide overall balance.

There are, unhappily, all too many families that do not function successfully. They are unhealthy, or "dysfunctional," for many different reasons. But the single most common reason is this: One of the parents is a substance abuser—be it of alcohol or other drugs. One out of every five families in America has an alcohol-addicted member. Yours may or may not be one of them, but the fact that you are reading this book means that you are probably concerned about one of your kids—and the only way to deal with that concern is to face it, by learning all you can about chemical dependence.

A Disease of Denial

Joanie was eleven when Bill first saw her in his pediatric office. She said she'd been having stomach pains, which turned out to be mild enough to be treated with a simple medication. A month later she was back with a complaint of headaches. The third time she came in feeling sick, Bill asked her gently, "Joanie, who's drinking at home?" The tears flowed. Sure enough, we learned that her father was a traveling salesman with a drinking problem, and Joanie's physical upsets were a direct reflection of the pain her father's return home always caused her.

Sadly, if not surprisingly, a few years later Joanie developed a drinking problem of her own.

When one family member is drinking, everyone else is affected by it. One drinks and the others react—most often by denying that a drinking problem exists. Alcoholism is a disease of denial: Oftentimes, both the drinker and the spouse will hide the facts, hide the bottles, and distort the truth, while the spouse takes on the responsibilities of both partners. Children, trying to alter their behavior to suit one or both parents, suppress their fears, swallow their anxieties—and develop ways to cope that can create both physical and emotional problems for them then, and later in life as well. In the anger and anguish of adjusting to an addict's disruptions, everyone suffers.

Although Joanie's mother had tried to cover up the parental drinking problem, Joanie knew the truth—and her physical ailments were her reaction to the denial and confusion.

A CHILD NEVER KNOWS
WHAT TO EXPECT

Nearly 60 percent of the alcoholics in this country are the children of alcoholics. In our population today there are over 28 million children of alcoholics, approximately 6,600,000 of whom are under the age of 18. Chemical dependency is often passed on to the next generation: There is no longer any question but that there is a genetic factor involved in alcoholism. Whether raised within the alcoholic home or by someone else, the male children of alcoholics are five times as likely to become alcoholics themselves; the females, twice as likely. Female children of alcoholics are also likely to marry alcoholic men—thus perpetuating alcoholism's effects onto their own children.

The alcoholic home is characterized by fear, tension, and insecurity. Children never know what to expect when they come home from school—or what the evening will be like. Will the drinking parent be withdrawn and angry or warm and affectionate? Will he or she pass out on the couch? Will he or she someday get hit by a car or be injured or killed in some other way? Kids worry about the fighting that goes on at home, about whether there'll be any dinner, about whether or not they'll be able to concentrate on homework.

Children in alcoholic households are never free from anxiety about the chaotic situation that surrounds them. Inconsistency is the constant rule: What was allowed yesterday is forbidden today. Rules are always changing—bedtimes, curfews, TV-watching hours—the most mundane routines are always in flux. One or both parents can be kind one moment and furious the next. Children never know whether they're going to be facing the good parent or the bad one.

If a drinking parent is physically present but emotionally absent, how is a child to know that it's the result of that parent's blood alcohol level? Exposed to a drinking parent's drunken delusions, a child may believe the parent is actually going crazy. Behavior that's physiologically caused is often interpreted by children as deliberate cruelty.

Promises are made and broken. We all know how bitterly disappointed kids are when parents fail to show up at school events, for example. Unable to know for sure whether a parent is lying or making excuses, children in an alcoholic home all too often see *themselves* as the cause of the drinking; they may be convinced that a father wouldn't drink if they would only do better on math tests, or that a mother is drinking because she caught them teasing a younger brother or sister.

Conflict, blame, anger, and guilt are always present in an alcoholic household. Children, feeling both responsible and insecure, can't understand the role of the sober parent, who also seems to act crazy by reacting to the alcoholic, ignoring the youngsters instead of giving them support or protection. Kids are often angry at the sober parent for allowing the alcoholic to behave the way he or she does, or for not getting them another, better parent.

ROLE-PLAYING
FOR KEEPS

Five classic phases mark an alcoholic's deterioration: Denial, Rationalization, Isolation, Personality Change and Physical Decline. As the alcoholic parent moves along this progression, all other family members develop identifiable variations of the same set of defenses and symptoms. If the alcoholic goes untreated, each member of the family goes "down the same drain."

To outsiders, children will deny a parent's alcoholism and rationalize aberrant behavior. Jake, the 12-year-old son of an alcoholic parent, told us: "It wasn't the booze that made [my dad] do that—he was acting crazy because he has an electrolyte imbalance." Kids share their alcoholic parent's increasing isolation and, mirroring the alcoholic's physical deterioration, they show up in pediatric offices—as Joanie did—with multiple, though usually minor, physical complaints.

The children in an alcoholic family typically adopt certain characteristic roles in an effort to maintain some sort of balance in their badly skewed lives. These "survival roles" are all part of a valiant attempt to help the family survive with the least amount of discomfort for everyone.

As you'll see from the chart reproduced in the appendix (Appendix 2), the *family hero/heroine* is a Type A kid who grows into a Type A adult. Aiming for perfection, these kids are likely to fool us about their real feelings of inadequacy.

The *scapegoat*'s role serves to turn attention away

from the real problem. These youngsters tend to be sullen and defiant, and their behavior frequently progresses to the point where they develop a chemical dependency of their own. In one sense, the scapegoat's role is the most adaptive, since the kid's public persona conforms pretty closely to his or her real feelings.

The *lost child* affords the family some relief, since this is the child who isn't "there" to worry about. These kids survive by remaining invisible. They hide their anger and depression well, but often pay the price for it with severe emotional illness later on.

The *family mascot*, who plays the fool to divert attention from the problem-ridden grown-ups in the household, is a jokester who's not taken seriously, and who is most likely to be misdiagnosed. The near-hysteria of these youngsters is often mistaken for hyperactivity.

Keeping the Family Secret

Whatever their roles, the children of alcoholics learn early not to expect getting anything worth having, and not to trust anyone—either because they think they don't deserve to be treated well or because they expect that other people will always disappoint them. Trying to gain some control over their lives at the same time that they're reacting with hurt or anger to their home situation, children of alcoholics develop an almost pathological need for independence, which is based on their fear of ever having to rely on others. Learning to take care of their own needs, never trusting others to help them, they exhibit self-reliance born of necessity. But later in life, when they'd like to tell someone how upset they are about something, they just can't bring themselves to do it—and they may go out and drown their troubles in drink instead.

Children in an alcoholic home don't appeal to outsiders for help because parents transmit the message that they've got a family secret—a secret too awful to share with others. Admonitions are common: "Don't tell Mom about the beer you saw me drinking in the garage" or "When Uncle John comes this Christmas, don't tell him Mom is drinking again."

This need to guard the family secret keeps kids isolated from others and inhibits their ability to make friends or have fun. Most kids want their friends to sleep over, or to come over for dinner, or to join them for a party, or just to hang out in the playroom with them. But having to hide someone at home inevitably affects how much they can have friends over—and how much they can go to friends' homes, when they feel they can't return the invitations.

Some children show the effects of living with an alcoholic while they are still children: They fail in school or have psychosomatic illnesses or begin to abuse drugs or alcohol themselves. Others don't show the damage until later on. Sometimes it's not until midlife that adult children of alcoholics become depressed or display emotional problems that are directly attributable to the kind of childhoods they had. Recognition that the adult children of alcoholics may need help is a very recent phenomenon. The ground swell of that recognition is reflected in the thousands of self-help groups for what are now popularly referred to as ACOAs.

At 40, Jeff B. still has painful memories of the day he got taken to the circus. At two in the afternoon, his father was already drunk, so his mother refused to go with them. Jeff went off with just his father—and had a wonderful time. Later, still excited about the fun it had been, Jeff began telling his mother about it—only to have her give him a sudden hard slap across the face. At six, Jeff was used to being beaten by a drunken father, but now he saw that his mother was someone to be afraid of, too. "I got her message, all right: It wasn't okay to have a good time."

Beating-up-the-kid is a common occurrence in alcoholic households. Jeff's mother, having had a tiring day and in no mood for Jeff's excited chatter, was unable to strike out at her husband, so she took her resentment and frustration out on their child. Anger gets passed on like a family heirloom, and if the cause of the anger isn't addressed at the time it occurs, it creates difficulties for children later on.

By the time he reached his thirties, Jeff had developed both drinking and marital problems, and he suffered from a classic inheritance of the children of alcoholics: no self-esteem. After his marriage broke up, Jeff joined Alcoholics Anonymous and later an Adult Children of Alcoholics group. Repeatedly hurt and neglected as children, ACOA members try to understand their pasts in order to live more comfortably in the present. They share painful memories of how they learned to hide their real feelings, of how they were never able to trust. If ACOAs don't come to terms with their childhoods, they are in danger of repeating the family history of drinking or drug problems—and they're also more likely to develop eating disorders.

The biggest problem for many ACOAs is that they tend to live isolated lives. Since they grew up learning never to talk to anybody about what was going on at home, they begin to think that what's happening to them as adults is happening only to them. Joining ACOA, they feel an immense relief at discovering that they are far from being alone. Among other things they have in common are bad marriages, few friends, and difficulties on the job.

"For someone to grow up without having had a real childhood is a terrible loss," says Jeff. "I wanted, as an adult, to have all the things that I wanted as a little kid—love, affection, laughter—but they weren't just automatically there for me." One of the lessons Jeff had to learn was that he couldn't wipe out or change the past by ruining his present life with drink and marital discord and a nagging sense of failure.

"For years," he says today, "I carried around the belief that my parents had had love and affection within them but that they had held them back from me. Now I realize that there was just *no way* they had ever had those feelings. And I see that if I want those capacities—of loving, caring, sharing—I have to develop them on my own."

The Grown-Up Players

What *of* the two adult principals in an alcoholic household? The drinker, whether it's the mother or the father, is likely to be righteous, demanding, aggressive, rigid, a perfectionist about the behavior of other members of the family, grandiose, manipulative, and often charming—in an effort to get his or her own way. That sums up the patterns of behavior, but what the alcoholic actually *feels* is pain, guilt, hurt, shame—and fear.

The spouse of an alcoholic is the family's chief enabler: the one who allows the drinker to go on drinking by making excuses for him, covering up and caring for him, and generally assuming his responsibilities. Whether the enabler is the husband or wife, he or she is an understandably angry person—an over-responsible super-worker with a low sense of self-worth. Feeling victimized by not being able to control the alcoholic or the drinking, the enabler suffers rejection, self-pity, self-blame, a sense of powerlessness—and a great deal of pain. He or she lives for the day when the drinking spouse finally sobers up . . . or even dies. Either way there is hope that it will end the pain.

MAKING UP
FOR IT

If you grew up in such a household, everything we've said so far has probably rung a bell of unwelcome recall. And the likelihood is that when you married you took a vow to make things different for your children: No matter what, you resolved, your kids would have all the love and support and protection that your own child-hood didn't afford you. As a child, you were robbed; as a parent, you swore to make up for it.

"When I was a kid," says Althea D., a mother who came to us because her teenager is on drugs, "it seemed to me that my alcoholic mother was drunk almost all of the time. I remember coming home from school one day in tears because I hadn't made the glee club, but she didn't sit down and put her arm around me and say, 'Gosh, that's hard, that's tough to take, no wonder you feel bad.' No, I remember to this day that what she said, hardly even bothering to look at me, was, 'Your sister is driving me crazy.' The answer I got to my problem as a kid was my mother's adult problem.

"Neither my sister nor I ever got an appropriate

answer to any question we asked. Nobody gave us any tools for problem solving. We just made our muddled way through childhood without any help from either Mommy or Daddy.

"So when I got to be a parent I was going to be loving and understanding and always there when my kids needed me; I wasn't going to let them suffer the pain and the loneliness that my mother laid on me. And what happened? As a parent I gave in to anything and everything my kids wanted—not only because I loved them but also because I didn't want to take the risk of having them not like me. That wasn't exactly appropriate parental behavior either, was it? I bent over backwards to make everything nice for them because I didn't know, from my own upbringing, what a parent *should* be.

"And so my husband and I, trying always to do the best we could, have managed to raise a kid who's in trouble with drugs. We just hope to God it's not too late to help him. . . . I feel so guilty.

George L. came to us because he was worried that Lisa, his 13-year-old, was "turning into a pothead." In our initial interview he told us that he'd grown up with an alcoholic father. "He never missed taking me to a baseball game, or a football or basketball game, either, but he just used these outings to get plastered. He'd drop me back at home and then go off to a bar somewhere to get even drunker. The whole time I was growing up, he never once sat down and talked to me in any meaningful way. Boy, was I determined to make my own fatherhood different!"

Things didn't turn out that well for George's ambitions as a parent: Hilary, the girl he married, was a confirmed alcoholic by the time she reached her thirties.

"But I could never bring myself to say to our older kids, the boys, 'Are you concerned about Mom's drinking?' No, I helped them turn it into a family secret: 'Mommy isn't feeling well,' I'd say, 'so she's going to lie down and rest for a bit. We'll go swimming so she can lie there and get better.'

"I was paying for Hilary to see a psychiatrist because I thought that might help, but her weekly appointment was early in the morning—she'd be sober enough when she saw the doctor, so how was he to know that she'd come home and be drunk by noon?

"Now there's Lisa, our baby, and I have this sick feeling that she's going to keep up her end of this old family tradition."

AIMING FOR
PERFECTION

For most jobs in life, there's a training period—when you're new at something, nobody expects perfection right away. But for one of the hardest jobs in the world, parenting, no introductory course is offered: There you are with a baby, so that makes you a parent. There are lots of how-to books you can read, of course, but hands-on experience is really the only way to learn.

All the books in the world won't help you to understand that there is no such thing as perfect parenting—we can spend an adult lifetime on the job and come out of it rank amateurs. One of the things we do learn eventually, at least, is that even those of us who had two perfectly sober parents cannot provide our kids with all-encompassing love and happiness. Parents who think they can are simply misguided.

This need to give our children more than we had as children, to make life nice for them, easy for them, has made for a lot of spoiled children—and experience has proved that they can get in trouble just as fast, sometimes even faster, than kids who aren't doted on. There are times when the best thing you can do for kids is make it tough on them. The lives they have as adults will present them with one frustration after another; how are they going to handle themselves as frustrated adults if they haven't learned to live with frustration while they're kids? If you've always given them what they want, they'll always expect, for the rest of their lives, that someone else will smooth the way for them. And if some*body* doesn't, maybe some*thing* will. Relief is just a swallow away . . .

NOT IN YOUR HOUSEHOLD

But let's suppose that you grew up in a family untroubled by the presence of an alcoholic. The closest you ever came to meeting one in the family was your brief introduction to old Uncle Homer, whose reputation as a skirt-chaser was far more interesting to you than his reputation for tippling.

Nor is there an alcoholic in your present household—or not a declared one, anyway. But has anything you've read so far made you a little uncomfortable about the drinking you and/or your spouse do? If so, there's a very simple drinking-problem test you can take for either or both of you—silently, as you read along. It's called the CAGE test, and here it is, letter by letter of the acronym:

C stands for Cutting down on drinking. Have you, or your spouse, ever tried to do so? Has either of you ever switched from martinis to wine or beer in an effort to cut down? Or vowed to have only two drinks—and then had three?

A is for Annoyance. Has anyone ever irked you or your spouse by questioning your drinking? Has it ever made you angry to have someone suggest that "since you've had a few," they'd be glad to take the driver's seat? Have either you or your spouse been disappointed by the other's drinking behavior—enough so that when the subject was raised one of you got annoyed, maybe even angry?

G is for Guilt. Has drinking ever made one or the other of you do something so foolish that you felt guilty about it later? Maybe you yelled at one of the kids for doing something that in the cosmic order of things really wasn't much of a crime—did you feel guilty about the yelling later, when you were sober?

E is for Eye-opener. The need is not necessarily for a morning drink, but for four or five cups of coffee and a few pills, say, for you to get going in the morning after the night before. (Is it possible that the great success of the Sunday brunch in this country is due not to its fulfilling a societal need, but to its giving so many people a reason to have a hair of the dog that bit them Saturday night?)

Answering "yes" to two of the four categories in the CAGE test makes the odds nine-to-one that an adult in

your household has a drinking problem. If you haggled
with yourself as you took this test about what an honest
answer was, perhaps it's an indication of denial.

But if both you and your spouse passed the test with
flying colors, it's probable that you can identify with one
or another member of the following households:

The Nonalcoholic Household

Meg J., a school psychologist, and Harry, a highly paid
chemist with a pharmaceutical firm, enjoyed their
material success and enjoyed their children, too. As
parents, they were good to Caroline and Mickey but
"sensible" when it came to refusing them the extras that
kids yearn for but can just as well do without. Harry's
passion was his sailboat, which was often the setting of
family togetherness in the summers. Another of Harry's
passions was beer, though he drank only on weekends
and never exceeded four cans a day. Meg occasionally
drank Scotch, bringing a highball into the living room
after she'd gotten dinner started in the kitchen.

The summer Mickey turned 15 he started making
excuses for not joining the others on the boat. That fall
he seemed uninterested in school, uninterested in his
family, and uninterested in the friends he'd grown up
with. As Harry put it to us, "He traded in good friends
for bad ones—I wouldn't have trusted any of them for a
minute." Mickey went from earning As to getting Cs, and
when Meg found drug paraphernalia in his room, she
and Harry lit into him about it.

"He promised to quit," Harry said, "but the only
thing he quit was doing drugs in his room. What the hell
have Meg and I done to deserve this?"

* * *

Sally G., a commercial artist, and John, an engineer, were the parents of 13-year-old Judy and six-year-old Sam. They were nondrinkers, but kept a liquor cabinet stocked for occasions when friends and neighbors dropped in, and served wine at the dinner parties they gave. Grossly overweight, Sally, had she taken the CAGE test in terms of her addiction to food, certainly wouldn't have passed. Always concerned, as addicts are, with supplies, Sally noticed one day that the liquor in the house was starting to go fast: First there was a sizable drop in the level of vodka, and then the bourbon. She relayed her suspicions to John and he was dumbfounded at her suggestion that Judy had been drinking. "Sally, you're crazy—she's only in the eighth grade!"

Sally wasn't crazy.

Joyce H. and Bill H. had six children between them, four in the same household: Joyce's two from a previous marriage and two of their own. Bill's two kids, from *his* previous marriage, lived in another part of the city but often joined Joyce and Bill and Danny and Steve and Melinda and Jane on weekends. Joyce really enjoyed the two-day crush, but it drove Bill a bit nuts. By Sunday evening, when he delivered Bill Jr. and Nan back to their mother, he was ready for what he called a good stiff drink. He usually had two of them before sinking gratefully into bed at the end of the day.

Weekends were sometimes trying but always manageable; vacations with this "blended family" were another matter. Joyce stayed serene in the center of all six children for the two weeks they spent at their summer cabin in the woods, but Bill always wound up being more protective of Bill Jr. and Nan than he really had to be: The kids all got along together for the most part, but Bill worried that *his* two were somehow going to be given short shrift by the others. At the close of the day, it was two, sometimes three, good stiff drinks.

Going into the cabin kitchen to fix himself the first drink one evening, he caught Bill Jr., 13, in the guilty act of swigging from the bottle. Bill Sr.'s reaction was murderous: "Is that the kind of thing your mother lets you do at home these days? Get the hell away from that booze and *stay* away from it! No more vacations here with us, buster, if that's a new habit you've got. Just wait till I talk to *her* about this!"

Patsy R. was a single parent, a divorced school-teacher bringing up Timmy, a high-school sophomore, and Jill, a third-grader. A fourth member of the household was Dennis, a lawyer who'd moved in as Patsy's companion when her divorce was final. Jill loved Dennis and Timmy all but worshipped him: Dennis turned out to be all the things Timmy had wanted from a real father who'd been unable to supply them. The foursome made a good family—until Patsy and Dennis discovered that Timmy had picked up a pot habit at school. When Patsy tried to reason with him about the harm he could be headed for, Timmy told her to get off his back—that "everyone else" smoked pot and that he didn't want to hear any "preaching" from her about it. The next time Timmy came home discernibly stoned, Dennis sat the boy down and said, "Look, son, we don't like what's happening with you, and—" In mid-sentence Timmy got up and walked off, saying angrily over his shoulder, "Someone who isn't my father better quit calling me 'son'!"

* * *

A good student, a promising piano player, a pretty child at 14, Ginny was the delight of her parents' life. A year later, Bob and Elaine P. were in despair over her. They hadn't liked the fact that she'd suddenly gone in for "looking tarty," as Bob put it: a lot of heavy makeup, pendulous rhinestone earrings, and short slit skirts. But they swallowed their feelings and said nothing because they thought adolescents had a right to try out their newfound sexuality. They swallowed further disappointment when Ginny announced one day that she was through with the piano—her lessons were a bore.

What upset Bob and Elaine more than anything, though, was the boyfriend Ginny acquired. They never saw him in anything but a torn T-shirt and scruffy jeans, a cigarette perpetually dangling from the corner of his mouth. Mostly they didn't see him, period. He'd pull up in front of the house in what Elaine called his "automobile wreck" and honk the horn for Ginny to join him.

She never got home from these dates when she was supposed to, but she never ran out of excuses, either: "The car broke down" or "The concert started late" or "We had to drive this girl home."

Her behavior was unpredictable: Sometimes, coming home from a date, she'd be cheerful and talkative; other times she'd run straight up the stairs to her room and slam the door without so much as saying hello. During her periods of despondency, her parents would let her escape from household chores and stay in her room for hours at a time, worrying between themselves about her depressions and wondering what on earth caused them.

Then Bob and Elaine began missing money from their wallets. When they called her on this, Ginny burst into tears and tried to make them feel guilty for her having to steal from them "because everyone else gets more money than I do."

"We were so damn gullible," Bob recalled. "We thought she was upstairs crying her eyes out, but all she was doing up there was drugs."

It's important to state again: Kids who do drugs or drink alcohol can come from so-called "normal" families. The pressure to use is all around them—and adolescents are particularly vulnerable.

If you thought it could never happen to your kid . . . you're not alone.

4

IT'S ALL IN THE WAY YOU LOOK AT IT

ATTITUDE ADJUSTMENT

The photograph in the ad is of a boy who can't be more than 13, bending over a line of cocaine laid on the surface of a mirror. The headline reads: HE'S THE IMAGE OF HIS FATHER. The caption says: "People who turn kids onto drugs aren't always the dregs of the earth. They're people who love children more than anything. Parents. Everything mothers and fathers do, no matter how discreet, leaves a lasting impression on sons and daughters. With millions of parents doing drugs, it's no wonder millions of kids are doing the same. If parents stop, kids won't start."

A variation of this ad, appearing now on full pages of newspapers and magazines, shows a photo of an adult, lifting a tiny teaspoon to his nostril. The headline reads: HOW DO YOU EXPECT YOUR KID TO KEEP HIS OR HER

NOSE CLEAN IF YOU DON'T? The caption: "They're the worst kind of hypocrites: parents who warn their children about using drugs while they themselves are abusing drugs. What parents don't seem to realize is that it takes more than a good sermon to keep kids on the straight and narrow. It takes a good example. Without it, kids are likely to wind up abusing drugs just like Mom and Dad. If you want your son to be strong, if you want your daughter to have the willpower to walk the other way, practice what you preach. Because you can't control your children if you can't control yourself."

Pretty strong stuff, isn't it? The ads are paid for by an organization called Partnership for a Drug-Free America, which is certainly to be commended for its parent-jolting campaign on the theme of a child's attitude: If you do it, why shouldn't I?

You don't need the kind of jarring these ads provide or you wouldn't be reading this book. You are already aware that there is, or may be, a problem and you want to help your child. To be able to do that, you first need to examine your own attitudes about chemical dependency. They may require adjustment.

ATTITUDE #1: DENIAL

Denial, which we've mentioned briefly already, is the single most important attitude for you to look at closely. In an addictive situation, the family tries to control the addict, the addict tries to control the family, the spouse tries to control against being controlled—everyone is involved in manipulative behavior to *deny the existence of a problem*. And the more evidence that piles up to indicate a problem, the more defensive everyone gets, the harder they work to keep up the facade of stability.

When a parent first faces the question "Could my child have a drug problem?" the denial sets in with the immediate answer: No! Not him, not her, not us, not in our family, not in this house.

When Claire and Harry came home from a dinner party late one evening, their teenage daughter, Cheryl, had already gone to bed.

They found a still-warm marijuana pipe on the living room coffee table. In spite of Cheryl's mounting school problems, unpredictable mood swings, and strange new friends, Claire and Harry believed their daughter the next morning when she said the pipe belonged to a friend. She never smoked that stuff, she told them.

Scott explained his third car accident to his mom and dad by saying someone had backed into his car while he was at a party in a nearby town.

He smelled of alcohol as he told his story.

Two months before this, he'd been stopped by the police for erratic driving and open beer cans had been found in the car. But now, as then, his parents had Scott's car repaired, set no new rules, and did nothing to curb his behavior.

It's natural for the parents of children who seem to be in trouble to feel guilt and embarrassment—which is what usually prevents them from seeking help earlier. That's why it's important to know that you as a parent did not cause your child's addiction. It is no reflection on how well you're doing your job—but, while you did not cause the problem, what you *do* or *don't* do can sure help it along the way.

Mothers and fathers, though usually in different ways, are often unwitting, unknowing, unsuspecting enablers for their children.

The Mother's Side

As a mother, you surely remember seeing your child off to nursery school or kindergarten that first time. Along with the pride you felt in his readiness for independence, you probably also felt a little tug of worry that he might still need your protection, and a little tug of regret that he might not. After all, you brought him into the world totally dependent on you, and from the very first you enjoyed that dependence, enjoyed being wanted, being able to fulfill his needs.

As a youngster enters adolescence, a mother may again find it difficult to release her child from the protection she's been giving him for a dozen or more years. At some point her maternal instinct (a perfectly valid and usually reliable mechanism) may tell her something's gone wrong. But if she doesn't know what that something is, she may make excuses for her child's behavior and blame his difficulties on others.

And so her denial begins. If the school sees a problem, she finds fault with the school. She clings to anything positive she's ever heard others say about her child: that he's a sweet boy, that he's nice looking, that he's kind to animals and considerate of the elderly. And all the while this paragon turns increasingly sullen, defiant, disrespectful, and withdrawn.

His mother, the enabler, likes to think "he's just going through a phase"—a phase that includes worsening grades, an indifference to curfews, and no regard whatsoever for either the feelings or the wishes of his parents.

Building defenses around her denial, the mother keeps trying to understand this child, denying the possibility that the rotten behavior could be linked to drug use. The harder she tries to reach him, the worse his behavior gets. She feels guilty and pained by her inadequacy, unable to bear the idea, the shame, of having a child "in trouble." She is both angry and afraid and feels somehow punished for not having been a good enough mother.

Looking for answers to what has become a family problem, she may turn on the boy's father and accuse him of having spent too much of his time on his job, and too little time on his child.

The Father's Side

Upset himself, the father responds with his own form of denial. He is likely to think that the boy's problem stems from too little disciplinary action taken over the years. Reciting examples of restrictions that weren't enforced, he fails to understand that rule-breaking is only a *symptom* of the problem, not the *cause* of it.

He, too, feels guilty about the way his son is turning out, reacting with anger toward both his wife and child. This, of course, produces the same reaction in his son that the mother's "meddling" concern does: further retreat into the euphoria that drugs produce for him.

The father, who can't seem to get anyone at home to listen to his ideas about "pulling up your own socks," feels powerless, lonely, and hurt as he watches the boy losing ground to whatever it is that's wrong. But let anyone outside the family suggest that his son might have a drug problem, and he'll become outraged and downright defensive. *That's* denial.

ATTITUDE #2:
SOCIAL STIGMA

One of the biggest deterrents against seeking immediate help for an addicted child is that in parents' minds, family honor is somehow at stake. But what on earth does honor have to do with illness?

Alcoholism has been accorded the medical definition of a disease in this country for over thirty years, yet there are thousands of doctors—even today, even young ones—who are reluctant to call this spade a spade. Their attitudes toward alcoholism were formed back when they were interns and residents. Drunks, thrown into hospitals in the middle of the night, were obstreperous pains in the neck and always seemed to arrive just when a doctor was trying to save someone else's life. There was never a reason to see the alcoholics who joined AA and got better—they saw only the returnees. "Him again . . ." "Her again . . ." "Damn."

And so a doctor's hesitation to make a diagnosis is born of knowing the "taint," the "shame," that still, in our supposedly enlightened society, goes with being labeled an alcoholic. Being called a drug addict isn't any different. Is "chemical dependent" a more acceptable term? Would fewer people flinch if the label was "substance abuser"? It makes little difference, really.

Our job is to knock off the labels and look at the facts: Drug addiction is a disease, just as, for example, diabetes is. If your genogram revealed that someone in your family had diabetes, and your child began urinating frequently and eating sugary stuff voraciously and losing weight, you'd get yourself to a pediatrician without wasting a moment. (Some parents are so alert to the possibility of diabetes that they bring soaked diapers in to a pediatrician and request urine tests.)

The Doctor's View

You and your doctor should keep in mind that alcoholism isn't a moral issue, that drug addicts are victims of a primary disease that's caused by a variety of biological, chemical, psychological, and sociological elements. You should know that an alcoholic is not a bad person who needs to be good but a sick person who needs to get well. You should know that in determining that your kid is an alcoholic, or a drug addict, or a chemical-dependent, or a substance abuser, doctors are making a *diagnosis*, not passing judgment.

Still, many physicians will avoid the diagnosis, if they see a way to do so, by choosing more acceptable diagnoses such as "minimal brain dysfunction" or "attention-deficit disorder." "Depression" and "borderline personality disorder" are other diagnostic "dumping grounds." So if, after examining your child, your doctor reaches such a conclusion, and you suspect that your child is using chemicals, you need to question the diagnosis. Failure to do so could constitute a danger to your child's health—and even to his life.

What you and the doctor need to keep in mind is that the greatest cause of death among this country's 15- to 22-year-old age group is accidents; and the greatest cause of accidents is alcohol and other drug use. What you also need to be constantly aware of is that this country has over three million kids under the age of 18 who are alcoholics or drug abusers. And what is the medical community doing about it? Not nearly enough. You can bet if there were three million kids with an attention-deficit disorder, we'd sure as hell be doing something about it.

Aside from a misdiagnosis, another serious way that your physician could inadvertently contribute to your child's drug problem is by overprescribing tranquilizers, amphetamines, barbiturates, and codeine-containing cough medicines—medications that have genuine usefulness but can lead to addiction. There are four categories into which we can put these doctors: the genuinely duped physicians, who are conned by drug seekers; the undereducated physicians, who haven't kept abreast of the medical implications of the drug problem; those few disabled physicians who use addictive drugs themselves; and, most regrettably, the tiny number of physicians who overprescribe for profit.

SOCIAL STIGMA PLUS DENIAL

For the most part, doctors are simply guilty of complying with the parental and societal attitude that if we call "it" what it is, we're rendering judgment—accusing, not diagnosing.

Most parents who come to our institute have kids who are already in trouble. These parents have put off "doing something about it" for as long as possible because they didn't believe, or didn't want to believe, that this was happening to them. What went on in their heads was that if they called someone for help, they'd hear a note of disapproval at the other end of the phone—a gasp, maybe, at the confession of what the problem might be. We get plenty of calls from people who don't want to give us their last names. The stigma attached to saying "I think my kid has a drug problem" admits, in their minds, the possibility of then having to say "I screwed up as a parent."

Who needs this attitude when a young person's *life* may be at stake? We try our hardest at the institute to get parents to come out of the woodwork and come in for help. To stop hiding, covering up, protecting—and courting disaster. And, sadly, the very people who are hiding are often the ones most in need of help themselves.

NOT OUR TOWN!

• A teacher notices that a B-average student spends time nodding off in class, and he further notes that during lunchtime this same student has begun hanging out with known drug users. The teacher says nothing about it to anyone. After all, he tells himself, he's a history teacher, not a cop.
• A police officer sees a 16-year-old boy making a drug deal on the street. The cop turns his head away from the scene because just last week he'd been at a men's club meeting with this kid's father and had confronted him with his suspicions that the man's son was on drugs. The cop had been politely told to mind his own business.
• A judge, knowing that jails are overcrowded and dangerous places, sentences a second-time offender for drug dealing to a one-year probation and suspends the fine.

• A pediatrician treats a 13-year-old girl for a sinus problem and a cough by giving her an antihistamine. He doesn't ask her if she's using cocaine or crack because he feels that would weaken their doctor/patient relationship.

A community is a macrocosm of parental views: It reflects all the jealousies, all the fears, all the attitudes you find in a household. Like parents, communities are concerned with their good reputations. Often, a school with a known drug problem defends itself when accused and declares it's in "fine shape—so go pick on some other school that's worse." People in a community who pay high taxes to support schools don't want to be told, after spending all that money, that the schools have kids with problems.

Parents in a well-heeled community who hear rumors that the local school their kids are attending has drug problems sometimes yank their kids out and send them to a "better" school, and if necessary take them out again and dispatch them to the "best." So the kids play musical schools and discover that in private schools there's just as much and maybe more drug use because there's more student money to be spent on it—and the quality of the drugs available is upgraded as they go along from good to better to best.

Here's another dismaying attitude shared by parents and the communities they live in: Even suicide does not carry the same social stigma that drug dependency does. (We're not talking about grief, but stigma.) Adolescent suicides can occur in clusters. When a community is hit by one such cluster, it touches off demands for panels and lectures and symposiums on the subject. Droves of worried parents attend because the immediate and natural fear that suicide engenders is "Could our kid be next?"

Just try to get that same community, however, to attend a panel or a lecture or a symposium on teenage drug abuse (which is almost always involved in teenage suicides) and parents *stay away* in droves because they're all saying "Not *our* kid!" A town concerned with its reputation may allow the pain to go on and on rather than open itself up to discussions of the problem—discussions that could lead to solutions and allow healing to begin.

IT'S ALL IN THE WAY YOU LOOK AT IT

• A 15-year-old girl sees her 13-year-old brother smoking pot on the way home from school. She doesn't tell their parents for fear her brother will retaliate by telling them "secrets" about her own sexual activities.

• A psychologist sees a teenager for several months because of behavioral problems. The girl admits that she uses drugs "sometimes." The therapist continues to see the patient without making abstinence a part of the ground rules. He doesn't want to upset the "therapeutic alliance." The teenager is often high at sessions; her therapist hopes to treat the drug problem by exploring the girl's "underlying" psychological problems.

If you want to adopt a new attitude about addictions, here's the best one you could have: It's the only fatal disease from which people can be guaranteed full recovery. All they have to do is stop what they're doing.

5

Warning Signs

IN SEARCH OF A DUCK

If you think there's a drug problem with your child, there probably is. You may already have picked up a warning sign or two. Usually one or two signs can't be considered much evidence—unless, of course, (1) you find your kid's drug stash or (2) you catch him or her in the act of using it.

YOU NEVER KNOW—
UNTIL YOU KNOW

Warning signs, taken separately, may mean nothing much, but added together they can amount to a lot. We have a saying about these signals that goes "If it looks like a duck, if it walks like a duck, if it quacks like a duck, it's probably a duck."

What you should look for is not a single sign but a *cluster of them*, not a single act but a *developing pattern* of behavior, not a single suspicious episode but a *series* of them. Parental instinct will probably tell you, perhaps quite suddenly and early on, when you're right to put two and two together—and come up with a duck.

Here, derived from our clinical experience with drug-abusing kids, are some of the signs that could mean you have trouble on your hands. (For a complete list of warning signs, see Appendix 3.)

1. A Change in Friends

Betty L., the mother of 15-year-old Candy, remembers: "The thing I noticed first was that I wasn't seeing her friends. When she was younger, everybody would come over, sometimes to stay for a while. There were five or six kids who were regulars at our house. Then one day it just seemed to me that we weren't seeing any of them anymore, and we didn't see much of her new friends, either. One or two of them were older; mostly, Candy would spend time with them on the phone."

Candy told us: *I didn't hang around with my old friends because I felt "less" than them. They didn't do drugs or even smoke cigarettes much. Drugging made me feel cool when I did it. It was real easy to find people who were doing drugs. In school, you just know. My mom had this thing about knowing my friends, so I'd bring them over once or twice and then I could say "I'm going to Jean's—you know, the girl you met a couple of weeks ago."*

* * *

Buddy's mother, Christine W., couldn't get over how "dumb" she felt when Buddy's father said to her in a rage one day, "Listen, don't you realize that those creeps he's hanging out with may not be members of the Mafia, but they sure as hell are dealing dope!"

It's perfectly natural for youngsters to be defensive about their friends when parental criticism—or even just inquiry—is voiced. *Oh, Mom, you just don't understand her! She's really cool—you just don't like the way she dresses.*

Kids will also respond in support if it's suggested that their new friends may use drugs. *So what? That's their business, isn't it? Don't worry, I'm not using*—they *are.*

Part of normal adolescence, as we know, is pulling away from the family to some degree, but if kids start using drugs, the pulling away becomes a vehicle to allow them to maintain the drug use. They create their own tight "family" of user friends, to the exclusion of others.

Buddy's mother told us, "When his father and I tried to find out more about who this Fred was, phoning at strange hours, all Buddy would tell us was that Fred's father was a dentist, and he'd reassure us that he was 'a really brilliant guy.'"

2. A Change in the Youngster Him/Herself

"Davy was the sweetest kid alive," his mother, Marlene P., told us, "and that's why we had such a hard time accepting the fact that he was turning into a kid who just seemed to be irritable all the time. We just couldn't imagine what on earth had happened to him to make him suddenly so unpleasant to live with. He was really nasty, even to Karen [a five-year-old sister]. I felt as if I never could please him, and neither could his father. If I said to him before he went off to school, 'What would you like to have for dinner tonight?' he'd shrug his shoulders and say, 'Who gives a shit?' His father finally couldn't stand it any longer and really let Davy have it one night, because in the middle of a basketball game they were watching on TV, Davy got up and switched the channel without even asking Jack if that was okay. Jack said, 'You just sit back down there, mister, and listen to *me* for a minute!' And in the middle of this lecture Jack was giving, Davy got up and just walked out of the house without saying a word, slamming the front door as he left."

Davy told us after completing rehab: *Just because I wasn't always in a good mood, they bugged me all the time, even my kid sister. I just wanted them all to shut up, to leave me alone for five minutes. I was smoking a lot of pot, then I got on speed and I spent a lot of time being uptight because I always worried about running out of whatever I needed. I guess I really did give them a hard time.*

"We never knew how Kathy was going to treat us. Everything about her was up in the air," her mother, Anne F., expains. "She could be so loving sometimes and we'd all get hugs, and then the next time she'd give us the cold shoulder, coming in and not even saying hello. What had we done to deserve this on-again, off-again stuff? Either way, you couldn't talk to her about it. I tried a few times and she would always say we were just making things up. She was so good at turning things around that we began to feel *we* were crazy. It was hard to put a finger on it."

Kathy told us after treatment: *They were always saying "What's the matter?" I just got so sick of them being after me all the time, I thought they were trying to find out stuff and make me confess. Joey and I were doing a lot of drugs—I knew when we went out that he'd always have something, hash or coke, and when he brought me home he'd always give me more to have in my room later. For a long time, you know, I didn't have to buy it for myself. I thought Joey was a real great friend.*

"There were two things about Jody that made her so special," her father, John R., remembers. "From the time she was really little she was the most lovey-dovey kid you ever saw, always wanting to sit in your lap, putting her arms out so you'd pick her up. And she was always crazy about stories and books, wanting you to read to her. When she got old enough to read herself, she was always buried in a book. Well, that changed. The summer before eighth grade she sort of didn't want anything to do with us. Once she even told me to get my hands off her—can you imagine? She quit reading that summer, too. Just spent her time staying away from the house, away from us."

Jody told us: *My drinking built up from the fun thing it was in the summer. I got caught drunk at school one morning. I finally told them in November that I was drinking the whole time. And I told them I'd stop, to get them off my neck, and they thought I stopped. I lasted two days.*

"Because we didn't want our kids to think they were something so special and that things would always be done for them," Sarah J. says, "they had regular chores.

Jimmy was supposed to carry the garbage and newspapers down to the basement of our apartment building every night, and clean the cat's litter box. Of course it wasn't anything he *enjoyed* doing, but he did it without fussing mostly. Then it got to be something I had to ask him to do, and then I had to *order* him to do it. He'd gotten so sullen about everything that seemed to remind him that he was a member of our family. One night at garbage time, I knocked on the door of his room to tell him and he yelled out, 'Oh, for God's sake, let Anna do it in the morning!' Anna is our cleaning lady. I thought Dick was going to get up and kill his own child when he heard that."

Jimmy told us: *I couldn't do just one. One led to another and another. I always needed more to get high—to stay high. My parents bugged me about taking out the garbage and, man, it drove me crazy. It really made me mad.*

"It wasn't that he was always such a sensitive kid or anything," says Jack R. "In our family we tease each other, but it's always in a good-natured way. When Tim started getting his back up about almost everything anybody would say to him, we thought, well, it's a phase. He got so oversensitive, he was so ready to snap. Once he was going out somewhere and Jane didn't think he looked very neat, his hair was tangled, and Jane said, 'Where is our wild-child off to now?' and Tim turned around and screamed at us from the porch steps, 'Mind your own goddamn business, will you? Since when do I have to comb my hair before I can leave this house?' It was so much rage, over nothing at all, really. We were upset, but we forgot it. Well, sort of."

Tim told us: *Some weeks I'd do only an eighth of a gram [of coke] all night. Some nights me and my friends would really get high and stay that way till we ran out. My parents kept bugging me. It made me mad. They got in my way—coke was my way.*

"It wasn't just that she wouldn't cooperate," Betsy's mother, Janet M. recalls. "Both kids went to camp in the summer. Last spring, Betsy refused to go. She wanted to stay home and just hang out. We didn't think that was such a good idea, so we took her with us when we went to stay for two weeks with Bill's folks in Michigan. Betsy wasn't just unfriendly, she was plain hostile. Her grandparents were shocked and Bill and I felt so damn guilty about what terrible parents we must be to produce this monster child."

Betsy told us: *That was such a bummer. They live in this little town that's near the lake and I was supposed to be so grateful to be in a place where I could swim. All I could think about was getting back home, where I drank beer at other kids' houses and smoked pot in my room alone. I also drank [my parents] liquor and they were suspicious I guess, but they didn't really know anything then.*

"Sharon used to tell me all her problems," says her mother, Mary S. "She'd come to me with questions about everything in her life: what should she wear, what should she say, what should she do, who should she ask. More than just mother and daughter, I thought we were sort of friends—I would tell *her* a lot, too. Then after ninth grade it all changed and I couldn't understand it and I was really hurt. It wasn't even so much that she didn't treat me like a friend anymore, she didn't treat me like anything, as if mothers didn't count, or you had to avoid them. Her father, too. He'd always had this my-little-girl relationship with her, and then after that summer she just wasn't anybody's little girl. Everything she did she kept a secret from us."

Sharon told us: *I'd always think, "I don't have a drug problem, I just like to get high." I was doing 'ludes, speed, pot, coke—you name it. I'd go anywhere with anyone to get something.*

"Jamie was always a polite little boy," reports his mother, Amy C. "One thing we thought we'd done right was to have kids know their manners. Then when things started to go wrong with Jamie—he was the oldest—when we began to think he must be sneaking drinks from the liquor cabinet, he got so he couldn't talk without using terrible language. One day he was with Mike in a drugstore where he used to hang out with his friends, and Mike heard the druggist say to the girl who works there, 'What do you suppose Badmouth wants today—some more breath-sweetener?'"

Jamie told us: *Sometimes when I came home I'd stumble or something and they'd say "What's wrong with you?" and I'd tell them I only had some beer so they wouldn't know about the hard stuff, too. I kept a bottle under my pillow, but I was always a bit afraid she'd find it, so I started keeping it in one of my boots in the closet.*

"We couldn't understand Jerry's wild moods," Jane T. tells us. "He'd go from being cheerful, maybe even a little too cheerful, to being so down, so depressed-like that we'd really worry about what was wrong. We'd try to get him to talk, but he'd just leave if he thought we wanted to be close. I was so scared I thought maybe he had a mental problem, because when he was feeling good he was so different, like two different kids. But he didn't want to talk about anything then, either—he'd just say, 'I'm fine, lay off, Mom.'"

Jerry told us: *Sometimes I'd want to punch her face in. Dad would at least leave me alone, he'd be talking to my brothers and sisters when I was around. I had such downers, really miserable, I'd want to die or have it kill me, but it never did.*

So—has your child turned irritable, unpredictable, unloving, sullen, oversensitive, easily provoked, un-cooperative, hostile, secretive, foul-mouthed, or more than just a little moody?

One thing they will all do, if they start using drugs, is distance themselves from you. In our experience, there's no such thing as a kid doing drugs who's also maintaining a close, loving, caring, and sharing rela-tionship with his or her family. They'll try to avoid family outings—picnics or trips or church functions or parties in a family setting.

And they'll often try to get out of family meals: Eating together is a form of intimacy, and they want no part of that if they see a way to escape. They pull away from communication that threatens to go deeper than a perfunctory level—there's no talking with them on a *feeling* level. If they have problems of any sort, they don't want to discuss them; they're reluctant to be engaged in conversation that will involve their emotions. If they can't simply pull away quietly, they're apt to snarl at you, or shout.

They take great exception to having their privacy

invaded: They don't want you in their rooms, they don't want you in the living room if they're watching TV there, they don't seem to want you in their lives at all. *Leave me ALONE, will you? Get off my back! What's it to you?*

What it is to you is worry. A lot of worry.

3. A Change in the Way the Child Looks and Feels

Has he or she gone from being relatively neat to looking sloppy almost all of the time? Have they begun to affect rock-star clothing styles that make them look as if they *could* be druggies? Is she wearing a lot of makeup, using a lot of cologne? Is he wearing an earring (not always, but often, an indicator)?

A kid who is doing drugs often develops unusual sleep patterns (she may come to the dinner table in a bathrobe) and/or unusual eating patterns (he didn't want any dinner at all, but you find him staring into the refrigerator at three in the morning).

Have you noticed any weight loss—or gain? Do any of the following signs or symptoms seem to apply to your child?

• a red or puffy face
• bloodshot eyes
• bags under the eyes
• bumps and bruises (from falling)
• sudden vision difficulties
• a stuffy nose
• sniffles
• chest pains
• tattoos
• frequent sore throats

• coughing spells
• frequent infections
• digestive problems
• lingering or frequent colds and flu
• tremors, nervousness, jumpiness
• dizziness, headaches
• depression
• insomnia
• loss of appetite
• loss of coordination
• changes in reflexes
• paranoia
• memory lapses
• bizarre behavior

4. A Change in School Attitude

"Jody was a kid who really loved school," her dad, John R., says, "from kindergarten on. We never had to worry about report cards. She always got the best in everything, except for a math grade once. She used to love doing papers and was always so eager to have us read them before she passed them in. Every English teacher she ever had told us how well she did, and two of them even said she was bound to be a writer someday. And now look at what's happened. She's so changed."

Jody told us: *It was easy to drink in school. I would pour some of their vodka or gin into an empty soda can and walk to school with it. As soon as I got there, I'd put the can in the same place in the schoolyard so I could get to it at lunchtime. No one ever picked it up or threw it away. The only extracurricular activity I had at school was drinking.*

*   *   *

"Jamie was never what you'd call a really good student, but he did okay," Amy C. says. "His sister Katie—she was older—she was the one in the family who got the good grades. When Jamie started complaining and said he hated school, we thought it might be because he didn't want to be in any competition with Katie. He complained about all his teachers, said they weren't fair. He said everything about school was dumb, even football. The year before he couldn't wait to try out for the team, and then this year when we asked him about it he said football was stupid and he wouldn't go out for it if they paid him to play."

Jamie told us: *I never could have even made the team. A lot of those guys smoked pot or drank but only on weekends. I didn't want to be cut off, any time.*

Janet R. remembers: "After that trip to Michigan we wondered if Betsy would ever get over the sulks. Rob came home from camp and he was really glad to be a senior at last. Betsy was going into tenth grade and there was trouble right from the start. She really messed up. She hated everything, the teachers picked on her, the classes were dumb. Her first report card was a pretty good indication of how she felt: D's and F's."

Betsy told us: *I went from smoking pot in my room to other things there, too. I did 'ludes and speed. We usually did our drinking at this one guy's house, in their family room in the basement. This guy's father must be an alcoholic or something. He was drinking so much of the stuff himself that I doubt if anybody noticed who was using what. As soon as any bottle was down a few inches, the old man would bring in some more.*

* * *

"Dick and I were resigned to the fact that Jimmy probably wouldn't do so well in school that year," Sarah J. explained, "but he did everything worse even than we expected. Trinity bounced him and his grades were so terrible we couldn't get him into another private school. So he wound up in public school with all the other kids on drugs."

Jimmy told us: *I hated Trinity, but public school was worse—the teachers were real goons and I had a lot of resentment at having to move schools. All it really did was change the kids I hung out with and that's where I started doing crack. Man, it was a hoot! I liked it right away. I knew I would get crazy with the stuff.*

According to Jane T., "Jerry just seemed to quit everything to do with school at once. He dropped camera club. And the band. And his grades went all the way down. He just didn't do any studying that we could see. When he seemed to be in one of his good moods he thought he could get by without having to do any work, and when he was feeling worse than low he'd say he was just too depressed to open a book."

Jerry told us: *At school I really decided life was a bitch. I mean sometimes I was jumpy and kind of nervy and all keyed up and I'd think, "Okay, I can really hear what this teacher's telling me," and then it would be like my mind had suddenly gone blank. I mean blank, just blank.*

"When Sharon started school she was a B student and we thought that was fine, said Mary S. We never pushed her to study harder because both her father and I were C students and we were glad she was smarter than we were. But then last year she'd come home from school and tell me she was going to study in her room and then she'd come into the living room and turn on the TV and just sit there staring at it for hours. I'd say, 'How about schoolwork, honey?' and she'd say, 'Okay, Ma, in a minute,' and then it would be time for dinner. When she flunked history and got a D in English, we got scared."

Sharon told us: *I was okay in school for a while. I would take stuff out to study at home, but that began to make me nervous just looking at them there, waiting for me. So I'd have a couple of joints and then I'd close the books and go watch TV and not worry about it. In gym one day the teacher asked me if I was okay, she thought I looked funny or something, and did I have a problem? I didn't like this suddenly, so I just said, "No, do you?"*

"Davy was always popular with the teachers," Marlene P. remarked. "They always told us we should be proud. When he didn't make it through biology, we said we didn't want him to be a scientist anyhow. God knows what he'll be now. He should be graduating next year, but here we are wondering if he'll even be able to make it through this year."

Davy told us: *My father was really pissed because I didn't try out for basketball. That was his game. I'm tall and a pretty good player, but I was too busy doing drugs to care much about anything else. My marks were way down. Most exam days I stayed home and told my mom I had a cough and a sore throat. And that was true, I was really telling her the truth.*

"The second time Tim 'lost' a report card," Jack R. informed us. "Jane phoned the school and they said perhaps she should come in and talk to Mrs. Carr, the vice principal. So she made an appointment to see this Mrs. Carr, and what a can of worms opened up. . . .

Tim had been skipping school for days at a time. He never made it to exams and never turned in any papers that were due. Jane took it really hard—I mean, why hadn't somebody from school gotten in touch with us and told us what was *happening*, for heaven's sake? When Jane asked Mrs. Carr why they had kept us in the dark like that, she just said, 'Well, we hoped Tim would get over his troubles enough to improve in school.' How do you like that? Here was a kid on drugs, we know now it was cocaine, and they didn't send us a word or pick up a phone. . . . What kind of sense does it make to cover up for a kid and not let his parents know what *they* must have known?" He paused for a moment. Maybe we didn't *want* to know, maybe we can't blame the school too much."

Tim told us: *I was doing a lot of drugs. I hardly knew where I was most of the time—at school or at home, it didn't make all that much difference. I felt so out of it.*

5. Missing Money or Personal Belongings

Parents pay for a lot of extras that are easy to reckon (and sometimes earn them a thank-you)—music lessons, camping equipment, ballet outfits. They shell out a lot, too, on The Allowance. The amount that your child needs or wants or receives may be more or less than what his or her best friend needs or wants or receives, but the differences don't generally promote serious family feuding. How or when or on what the money gets spent can seem baffling only to the childless; any parent learns soon enough that the amount of a child's allowance will never be considered enough and that today's treasures are tomorrow's cast-offs.

Money spent on drugs dissipates within seconds. We

know that an adult cocaine habit can take megabucks to support, but where do our kids get the bucks they spend for lesser glows? Undoubtedly out of their allowance pockets for starters, or out of what they earn from after-school jobs, but pockets are easily emptied, and then what?

It's not a pretty suggestion to make, and it's an ugly one to confront, but here it is. Kids tend to be generous with one another, and nobody's kid wants to be known as cheap. The warning sign we're asking you to consider now will take you light years beyond the mild embarrassment of having your five-year-old caught red-handed with the filched crayon in the stationery store. But if we are going to acknowledge hard truths, this is one we have to come up against: Could your child be living beyond the means you give to him, or beyond the means he earns?

Parents understandably tend to dismiss their own suspicions: If you notice a liquor-level drop or money missing, you may resolve to keep a closer eye on the household help, or even on younger siblings who can't seem to count beyond pennies. But what if—instead of waiting until a major appliance disappears—you did your teenager the ultimate favor of supposing that it's been *his* or *her* hand removing household money from the cookie jar? You just might, to everyone's ultimate relief, be taking the first positive step toward blocking an addiction that could ruin a lifetime.

We urge you again to think of warning signs in the plural, since they do come in differing sizes, shapes, and colors. Frank P. wondered why his 15-year-old daughter, Carla, returned home from the beach every day with a badly sunburned back. He never guessed it was because when you're stoned, lying face down in the sand is a natural position.

By the time he discovered Carla's secret and brought her to us, she was addicted to almost everything she had swallowed, snorted, smoked, and injected into her body for the previous two years. It didn't take much diagnostic skill to know that what we had on our hands looked like a duck, walked like a duck, quacked like a duck. . . .

If only one of Carla's teachers had noticed; if only her brothers hadn't protected her; if only her mother had been sober; if only her father had understood.

If only. What a terrible phrase to use in speaking of a young person's life.

6

RULES FOR

A HEALTHY FAMILY

DO YOURS GET BENT OUT OF SHAPE?

It might sound like locking the barn door after the horse has been stolen, but we think it's never too late to be mindful of the family mobile, and take notice of a jolt that could set off an unhappy chain reaction. And because some of the mobile segments could be younger siblings who are just beginning to feel the effects of family rules, we'd like to review some concepts that really should be rules laid down early in the upbringing of any family.

"USE YOUR FORK . . ."

No family can operate without rules. They might be bad rules—not always in effect, different for different members of the family, seldom enforced, rigid and inhumane, or so lax that they encourage the very behavior they are designed to thwart—but they are rules nonetheless. Even if unspoken.

Rules reflect the family that establishes them—its beliefs, its attitudes, its values. They change (for better or worse) according to what goes on within the family circle, as well as because of external events. Rules also help set the patterns of individual behavior that (fairly or unfairly) affect all other pieces of the family mobile. They can be as explicitly stated as "Use your fork and not your fingers," or they can remain covert or even exist as unconscious messages.

The very best rules are humanistic—they validate self-worth as they encourage individual growth to the benefit of all other members of the family.

You've almost certainly seen collections of parental tips in magazine articles, or in books, or even in brochures that adorn the table in your pediatrician's waiting room.

The problem with all such well-meant and generally sensible information is that while the examples often work well in families that are relatively stable, the fact is that most of us have hang-ups that interfere with making rules effective. The reality is that most of us don't know what a "normal" family is. We only know what we ourselves experienced as children, and we tend to follow—or deviate from—that example alone.

So when you come across some parenting expert's rules, you may give them a half-hearted try. But sooner or later you're likely to give up, on the basis that the regime just won't work in *your* family. Either the rules were too hard to enforce, or they were impractical, or it was all just too much trouble, anyway.

So in setting forth our rules here, we're taking into account the possible stumbling blocks to their success in *your* family.

An Ounce of Prevention Is Worth a Kilo of Cure

Rule One: Talk to your children about drugs and alcohol. When they come home with misinformation garnered from their peers, or when TV gives them the impression that drugs spell sophistication, you need to sit down with them and in a clear, nonjudgmental way share your own knowledge and expectations.

• But how can you talk to them about drugs and alcohol if you're not clear about the topic yourself? What *are* your attitudes about drinking and drugs? Think them through. Is a family drinker (even if it's Grandpa) already slanting opinions and feelings around your house?

Rule Two: Learn to hear. Communication should be kept free-flowing and open-ended. Show your kids as early as possible that what they say matters.

• Can you really be honest with your kid? If he or she told you something you were afraid to hear, how would you react? Do you block the possibility of hearing what you don't want to hear by being busy when your children try to talk to you? Can you share your *real* feelings with them? Your deep-down feelings? Or do you think immediately to yourself, "Well, no, I couldn't say *that*"? What about your own family secrets? Are you ashamed of any of them? If so, are you willing to at least talk about them?

Rule Three: Help your kids to feel good about themselves. Self-esteem is just as essential to growth as vitamins. Remember to praise efforts as well as accomplishments, and when it's necessary to correct, criticize the action rather than the child.

• How's your own self-esteem? We can't give away what we don't have ourselves. Did you get praised as a kid? No? Remember that it's not your fault if you didn't, but self-esteem gets passed along because it's *learned. How* did your mother or father praise you? Were you ever damned with faint praise? Are you repeating your parents' behavior?

Rule Four: Help them develop the right values—and set a good example. A strongly held system of ethical belief can give kids the courage to make decisions based on facts and positive convictions rather than on the misguided views and opinions of others. There's no such thing as reaching perfection in role-modeling—but you and your spouse can aim for it. Your own attitudes and your own drinking or drug habits will strongly influence your kids' ideas.

• What *about* your values? Do you bend rules to suit yourself? Does your car sport a fuzz-buster to alert you to cops on the highways? Do you cheat a little on your income taxes—and later brag about it? If a cashier somewhere gives you too much change, do you return it or pocket it? And again—what about your own drinking, since we're speaking of values? Is it truly in moderation? Do you and/or your spouse think it's okay to have an occasional joint?

Rule Five: Help kids deal with the pressures put on them by their peers. Small children often confuse being "gentle" and "loving" and being "a good friend" with a need to go along with doing whatever their friends are doing, and they often need you to help them "just say no."

• Do you generally do what your friends want you to? Do you feel comfortable saying no? Does it make you fearful of losing a friend? How often do you respond to social pressure by just saying no? How did your parents say no to you? How did they make you feel? What you learned from your world as a kid, right or wrong, is what you'll pass on to your own kids.

Rule Six: Set family rules about alcohol and drugs. It's always a good idea to be specific as well as stern. Let your kids know early what is acceptable behavior inside or outside of their home, and spell out the consequences of rule-breaking.

• Do you honestly believe your own rules are *right*? How consistent were your parents about rules *they* laid down? Were you ever punished for drinking or taking drugs? The rules of your childhood home are likely to be passed on to your own kids.

Rule Seven: Encourage healthy activities. Interests in sports, hobbies, school events, and music or dancing lessons will all help keep kids from having the time or the inclination to experiment with drugs or alcohol.

• Do you support your children's interest by going to watch them—or their friends—play ball or perform in a recital or act in a school play? Do you let them know these activities are important to you, too? *Are* they? What signals of approval do you send their way? What was your own experience as a youngster? Did one or both of your parents take an interest in *your* interests? Did you ever get the feeling they were faking their enthusiasm? What was important to you then? How do you feel about having fun now? What's your idea of relaxing? Does it include the presence of your kids? If it doesn't you may be letting them down.

Rule Eight: Team up with other parents. There are plenty of community groups out there for you to join, and they can be great reinforcement for the guidance you're providing at home. If your community *doesn't* have a parent-support group of some kind, start one. Check with other families about *their* rules—very few parents ever do this, which is too bad, because it's a highly effective way of parenting.

• Were you at the last PTA meeting? Did you go to a town meeting on drug abuse—or stay away because you were afraid it would be a signal to others that you might have a problem child at home? Are you fearful of checking with other families about their rules? Why? Because your kids would get mad at you? Or you'd embarrass them—or yourself? The strongest allies you can have are other parents. Work with them.

WHO'S GOT THE RIGHTS HERE, ANYWAY?

Sometimes a "just say no" philosophy of child-rearing isn't enough because it doesn't *go* far enough. More than just saying no is often needed; parents have somehow got to get their guts back. Somewhere along the line many of us abdicated and the kids took over—and so now we find ourselves faced with kids who think of college as a right, not a privilege. Kids who believe that having the family car is also a right, not a privilege. Kids who think that their rights should be the rules of the house.

Too often, if a child talks back to us, we tend to retreat, wondering what in the world we've done to earn the disrespectful treatment we're getting. Are so many of us really afraid to say no when we need to? How about risking a drop from favor by telling your kid you find his behavior intolerable? How about going even a step further by saying, "Hey, wait a minute, you're going to do this *because I said so*"? We understand that most of you vowed you'd treat your kids with more respect than your parents did with you; that your own relationship with your children would be based on openness and sharing. Our suggestions may go against every way you intended to handle your own kids, but in today's world it *has to be done*.

In a literal way, you bring home the bacon, you pay for the roof overhead, the gas and electricity, the clothes on everyone's back. Doesn't that earn you some rights? Is it your house or does it belong to the kids? If it's yours, don't you think you have a right to insist things be done your way?

So what about the concept of "child rights"? We know that, in general, children have few spokespersons to protect their needs and wants. But we are also firm in stating that these rights do *not* include the right to use a destructive chemical that endangers themselves, their family, their community. Drugs and alcohol kill and maim. Their use by children is against the law, and we do not support their "right" to use them.

Do we think a teenager has a right to confidentiality in his or her relationship to a physician? We don't think a physician has a right to hide a kid's drug use from his parents, any more than he or she has a right to hide the face that a kid's blood count indicates possible leukemia, or that his urine shows a possibility of diabetes. It's not a moral issue, or an issue of "rights," it's the issue involving *the diagnosis of a medical illness about which a parent has the right to know.*

Do we think it's ever okay to search a youngster's room? If indicated, yes. If you thought your child had a loaded gun, or cyanide pills, hidden in his room, would you search and remove them? Would you then face him with the evidence?

Drug use is serious business. Parents have both a right and a responsibility to protect their children. *Children do not have the right to destroy themselves, and we do not have the right to let them.* What we're talking about here is not how to enforce discipline, but how to save lives—not how to be popular with your kids, or how to be a pal, but how to be a parent.

Privacy is an important issue in any home. When your child has performed well as a functioning member of your family, you grant him privacy; he's earned it.

You retain the right, however, to question your own latitude in the matter if he does something to lose that trust. Were you too generous about letting him have his own TV, about borrowing your car? Has he abused your trust in any way? If he has, then you have a right to change his privileges accordingly. You are, after all, the governing member of the family.

A single incident of rebellion or bad behavior or indiscretion may not be reason to search your child's room, but you should certainly discuss that possibility with him. Not because you want the sword of Damocles to dangle above him but because you want to make it clear that his privileges have limits—and to indicate that you might have to measure them against your responsibility to protect him. If and when you've got strong reasons to suspect he's using drugs, a room-search *is* in order.

CONFIRMING YOUR SUSPICIONS

You probably already know what to look for: incense, marijuana seeds, joints, roach clips, rolling paper, bongs, pipes, razor blades, mirrors, straws, tiny spoons, bottle caps, stash cans, phony IDs or driver's license, invitations to booze parties and "happy hours."

Do you also know where to look? In back of stereo speakers, taped to the bottoms of dresser or desk drawers or to the backs of picture frames, in drapery folds or hems, in the pockets of almost-never-worn clothing, in the toes of old boots or shoes. If you've a reason to think it's alcohol you're looking for, you'll of course want to check your own liquor supply—but you might also check the inside of the toilet tank. (The most creative hiding place we ever heard about came from a kid who confessed it to us himself: he kept his stash in double plastic bags underneath the sand at the bottom of the family aquarium!)

Let's say you find a smoking gun. What do you do next—shoot from the hip?

7

STEPPING IN TO
STOP IT

MEET YOUR KID THE CON ARTIST

Collecting evidence is one thing. Confronting a kid with it is another. You know better than to do it when you happen to be angry, or when there's a sibling or friend within earshot. You need to plan, to set up a tribunal of sorts. And what you've got to keep in the front of your mind when you call it is this: *You're the one with clout; don't be afraid to use it.* You have appointed yourself/ selves judge, and this is not to be a trial by jury.

The confrontation is going to be painful, and you may feel that it will hurt you more than it does your child. But don't try to distance yourself: Show your feelings of genuine love and concern. Be calm, stay measured—and don't give an inch. Once more: You are in charge here.

How is your youngster likely to perceive this investi-

gation? You know as well as we do. She will pull back as
if this were a replay of the Spanish Inquisition. You will
be faced with someone who protests incredulity that
you've invaded her space. There will be tears of outrage
or pleading, perhaps. Hot denial. Lukewarm excuses.
Something like these:

EXCUSES	POSSIBLE RESPONSE
"It's not such a big deal."	This is a classic teenage-user red-flag response—an attempt to minimize. You could say "It is a big deal to me—it's your life."
"I only tried it once."	This is your chance to say "I won't tolerate it again," your chance to set the rules. He may have done it dozens of times, but let him know you won't tolerate it happening again— even one more time.
"We had a flat tire."	The kids themselves would be embarrassed if they knew how ancient an excuse this is. Your reply: "I'll check on it." (And be sure you do.)
"Why is pot any worse for me than liquor is for you?"	Another classic dodge to shift attention to you and away from her. A good reply is "I'm not the subject here—you are."
"I tried to call but you were out."	This may be reasonable, if you really were out, or not within earshot of the phone. Other-

	wise, it's probably nonsense. Your child is gambling that you won't pick him up on it. Pin him down with "When exactly did you call?"
"I just borrowed it."	You don't borrow a bong or a pipe unless you're planning to use it. A good answer might be "From who? Let's talk to him together."
"You don't really know my friends or you wouldn't say that."	Well, if you don't know their friends, you'd better make it a first order of business to get to know them. Remember that the wrong peer pressure, along with exposure to drug use, usually makes for drug use. Insist on meeting them!
"I'll never do it again."	A youngster may really believe what he's saying, but the hallmark of addiction is loss of control. If he has done it before, or does it again, you may have trouble on your hands. You could say "I believe you mean it now, but if it happens again, this is what we'll do. . . ." (State it clearly and stick to it.)
"But *all* the kids do it."	All what kids? Her friends? Can all the kids in town be doing it? Say firmly: "No, all the kids don't."

"Marijuana is harmless—everyone knows that."

The potency of today's marijuana is unarguable. Countless papers in scientific journals testify to the fact that this isn't true. State simply that "It isn't harmless" and have your facts handy as you face your youngster on this one.

"Somebody must have slipped me something."

Another time-honored excuse that doesn't excuse a thing. "I'm sorry, I don't believe you" is a clear message.

"Well, I've seen *you* drunk too, you know."

Again, an attempt to turn the spotlight off him/her and on you. (If his/her accusation is true, of course, you supplied the ammunition here.) Reply again: "I'm not the topic now, you are."

"I was holding it for a friend."

Why on earth would a friend hand over drugs for safekeeping? Answer your child with: "I find it hard to believe—getting you in trouble is not friendship."

"It was only beer."

Again, state the facts: Alcohol is alcohol. One can of beer equals one glass of wine equals one highball. A six-pack of beer equals a half pint of whiskey. So much for "only" anything.

"I didn't know *that's* what you meant."	Another attempt to confuse you with un-logic. Restate: "Yes, that's what I meant, you heard me." Don't let him or her off the hook.
"I don't see this as a big problem."	It is, or you wouldn't be reading this book. We cannot stress this enough. Let him know how important this is to you. Say "To me, it is a big problem, because I care about you."

SOME DEFINITE DON'TS WHEN YOU CONFRONT YOUR CHILD

- Don't fall for anything.
- Don't feel guilty. It's quite likely that you'll hear a variation of "If you loved me, you wouldn't do this to me." Don't accept the guilt trip your child is trying to lay on you. Your answer might be: "The fact is that I *do* love you—and that's exactly why I'm doing this."
- Don't argue. If you hear "But don't you *trust* me?" the answer is no, you don't. Trust is not something you hand out for free. A lack of trust does not mean a lack of love.
- Do not say "It isn't that I don't trust you, it's just that I worry." The fact is that you don't hand over trust until you think it's justified in certain situations. You would not trust a three-year-old to cross a busy traffic intersection alone; you would not trust a ten-year-old to pilot a helicopter. And you do not have to trust that your kid will make the right choice about drugs.

- Don't be conned into covering-up of any sort. Your child may not think of it this way, but he or she counts on your denying a problem. Do not replace checks or money lost, do not write excuses to teachers for late papers, do not pay to have a dented fender taken care of (it can come out of an allowance or from money earned in a part-time job).
- Don't protect your kid from feeling the pain of his or her own mess-ups. This is no time for "There, there, it'll get better." *Nothing* will get better until he or she has earned back your trust.

SOME DEFINITE DO'S

- Do lay down some new rules. You have as much right to insist on abstinence as you do the right to insist that a five-year-old take the antibiotic that's been prescribed for her.
- Do set firm curfews. Check with other parents, if you need to, on what seems both fair and realistic.
- Do establish party rules. Make sure there'll be an adult present, not just upstairs somewhere, but on patrol at all times.
- Do insist that no one who leaves the party will be let back in the house. Bottles can be hidden in bushes, and stashes in cars. Your kid may be mortified, and you may have to suffer through anger, but stick to your guns. Aren't lives being laid on the line? Some kids may stay away from your house, which might be all to the good.
- Do let your kids know you love them. Reassure your child of your support even though the rules seem tough. So many kids who've entered treatment have

said to us: "My parents never set rules. I thought they didn't care."

We were talking recently with the mother of a 16-year-old girl whose behavior was beginning to upset the whole family.

"I read that it was never too early to be concerned about drugs," this woman said, "but when should I get really worried?"

Right now, we told her. We had just seen her daughter; in reaction to our probes concerning the possibility of a drug problem, she had given us an elaborate shrug and said, "I can handle it."

That remark always means yes, there is a problem.

Acting upon it is another problem.

8

THE FOUR STAGES OF CHEMICAL DEPENDENCY

THE ONLY DIRECTION IS DOWN

You've recognized that your child has a problem. You've picked up on the warning signs, and maybe even found hard evidence of a drug or alcohol problem. But how do you know how "far gone" your child really is? When does "use" turn to "abuse," and abuse become "addiction?"

We know that curiosity, a sense of daring, and peer pressure are givens in adolescence. For most kids who "use" drugs and alcohol, their experimentation is limited to parties on weekends. Even that constitutes "abuse."

ABUSE

In this phase, drug use becomes problematic and damaging, but there is *still* an element of choice involved. Being drunk or stoned may be a frequent occurrence, but the abuser is still able to pull back and quit. Abusing kids are often surly, insolent, and supersensitive about themselves. They may erupt quickly and are often tyrannical in their households—everyone else in the family is manipulated into feeling guilty and accepting unacceptable behavior. Many abusing kids, on the other hand, can *look* okay, even as the abuse worsens.

ADDICTION

In this phase involvement with alcohol or other drugs is overwhelming, total. Once drug-taking has started, an addict can no longer control the amount used. Addicted kids are thus unmodifiable—they just can't stay shaped up. Remember, control doesn't mean not using or not drinking. "I can stop for a week at a time" is not evidence of control. An addicted kid cannot *consistently* choose when he will use or stop—and once started, he is in no control over the amount he takes. Kids like this don't respond to reason, punishment, or threats from parents, school, or society. The addiction is controlling *them*.

In Chapter Five, we considered a constellation of warning signs that present themselves at home and at

school when a young person is using drugs. For our
diagnostic purposes at the institute, we use a more
inclusive chart of "major and minor criteria for chemical dependency," which is reproduced in Appendix 3.
Also reproduced at the end of this chapter is our chart of
the progressive stages of chemical dependency, which
deserves some spelling out here. Originally described by
Vernon Johnson, and modified by Macdonald and
others, this chart defines drug and alcohol abuse as a
disease of feeling and behavior, comprising four stages:

Stage I: LEARNS MOOD SWING

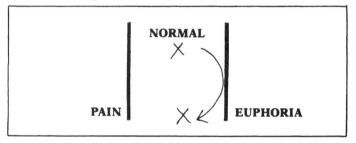

Experimenting, most often with tobacco, marijuana, or
alcohol, your child has discovered that his feelings can
be altered: It's possible (and easy) to go from feeling
ordinary to feeling *good*. He experiences mild guilt over
doing what he isn't supposed to, and will probably do
some moderate after-the-fact lying to you.

Once the youngster has felt the pleasure of a high
from using a certain drug, he'll find ways to repeat the
experience. At this stage the child can still get high, and
after use, return to feeling normal—"pain" isn't yet part
of the picture. In this phase, your child is likely to be less
dependent upon friends who offer her drugs—she has
her own supply now, which confers new social status

Stage 2: SEEKS THE MOOD SWING

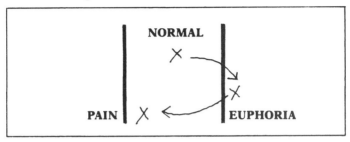

upon her. Finding that pot or alcohol isn't as "dangerous" as feared, the Stage II youngster may experiment
with prescribed pills in the family medicine cabinet—
tranquilizers, amphetamines, sedatives. Goals disappear, hobbies are un-cool, school is a drag. You might
notice:

erratic school grades	(Mary started the school year with an A in history but blew it by mid-term.)
skipping school	(classes and/or entire days)
extracurricular activities dropped	(John, an all-star middle-school basketball player, quits the freshman team, blaming the coach.)
family activities avoided	(Heather, who always loved family summers at the lodge in Montana, refuses to go this year.)
refusal to do chores	(Always cheerful about walking the dog, Joey now sullenly balks at the job.)

change in family communication	(Once eager to share her school-day news, Erica now sits in glum silence at the dinner table, eats and then leaves abruptly.)
unpredictable mood swings	(The once even-tempered Bobby is now cheerful one minute and explosive the next.)
conning behavior	(Laurie, hugging her Dad, gets her allowance despite the fact that she's just dented the car fender for the third time.)
feelings of depression expressed	(Refusing to get out of bed for school one morning, Barbara says to her mother, "I wish I was dead," and won't explain why she made the remark.)
frequent sore throats, red eyes, cough	(Sick for the fourth time this semester, Sandy complains, "It's my allergies," and her mother suggests for the fourth time, unavailingly, that they see the doctor.)
minor delinquent involvement	(Dennis and his pals get caught lighting fires in the dumpster behind the supermarket.)
no savings from an after-school job	(Colleen holds down two jobs, but her father overhears her borrowing money from her younger brother again.)

unexplained phone calls/visits from unfamiliar friends   (Rick's mother, upon answering the phone, hears only a click as someone hangs up. Rick's friends had always at least said hello to her before they asked if he was there.)

Stage 3: PREOCCUPATION WITH THE MOOD SWING/HARMFUL DEPENDENCE

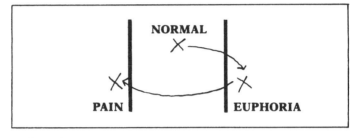

In this phase, your child experiences the feeling of pain, reached when euphoria evaporates. The pain of a hangover is treated with more of the drug, which gives him a sense of security, of comfort, of relief. At this stage it costs a certain amount of money to stay involved. A kid who has a job is likely to spend a lot of time at work. When not high, he is depressed, often feels ashamed of himself. Life seems like a bad trip. You might notice some of the following things, though not necessarily all.

school failure (more frequent skipping, possible expulsion)   (This can happen almost without your noticing it, and the progress toward expulsion comes without forewarning unless you're keeping a close watch. Don't blame the school—keep paying attention.)

vocal disrespect shown teachers in the classroom	(Don't ignore a kid's complaint about a fight with the teacher or the vice principal. You're only hearing one side of it when the kid says, "The teacher had it in for me.")
Amotivational behavior; lack of affect	(A kid's interest in everything seems to have evaporated. She can't be excited by anything in her young life—school is "boring" when it isn't "the pits.")
pathological lying	(You'd like to trust him, but you know in your heart you can't— the lies are blatant and outright. He hasn't looked you in the eye for weeks.)
rebellious dress styles; obvious awareness of messages from the drug culture	(Heavy-metal T-shirts with drug insignias, funky hairstyles, sudden tattoos, and, of course, leather jackets.)
police incidents: DWIs, stealing/ shoplifting	(Kids normally just don't do these things! Check it out at police headquarters—and don't let your kid con you into believing his defenses.)
money or valuables missing from home, a relative's house, or from the youngster's workplace	(Even piggybank money gets taken, along with stamp collections, stereos, radios, sterling silver. When a teenager needs drug money, he doesn't discriminate between friends, family, or strangers.)

| diluted or dwindling liquor supply at home | (Kids often tell us this was their first source of supply—"No one even noticed.") |
| "straight" friends dropped; companions now are losers | (What reason—excuse—has your child given you for dropping those earlier good friends you liked?) |

Stage 4: USES DRUGS/DRINK JUST TO FEEL NORMAL

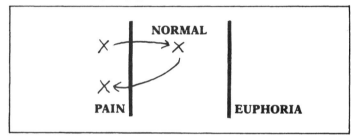

In this stage, euphoria is no longer attainable. A school dropout, the kid becomes a drifter, never able to get his act together. There is:

complete rejection of family values	(Alexis, once a cheerleader and choir member, is now plainly the town prostitute.)
paranoia; violent anger and aggression	(Ralph, rejected by his girlfriend, goes to her house and smashes windows with his bare fists.)
physical deterioration— weight loss, chronic cough	(The once healthy and athletic Maxine is now a gaunt and dirty version of her former self.)

repeated drug busts, jail sentences	(Seventy percent of the crimes committed by adolescents are drug-related. Tony's conviction for aggravated assault is the result of his fourth fight in two weeks.)
no friends	(Jobless, isolated from everyone he ever knew, Rich still hangs out in a suburban town just a few miles from the one in which he grew up.)

It's important for you to remember that no single characteristic can be taken for a diagnosis. In fact, certain characteristics, scattered throughout the chart, might not add up to a chemical-dependency problem either, but the *cluster*, or *groupings*, of characteristics, interpreted in the whole by a trained professional, can lead to a definitive diagnosis.

Such clusters, though perhaps obscure to you as a parent, should at the very least require referral to a specialist in chemical dependency.

There is no Stage 5 in this disease. The only alternatives a continuing user faces are insanity or death.

Or both.

THE PROGRESSIVE STAGES OF CHEMICAL DEPENDENCY WARNING SIGNS

Stage 0: CURIOSITY

- "Do-drug" environment
- Peer pressure—need for acceptance
- Adolescent curiosity plus willing to take risks

Stage I: LEARNING THE MOOD SWING

- Experimenting
- Mild Guilt
- Moderate after-the-fact lying

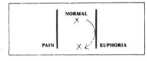

Stage 2: SEEKING THE MOOD SWING

- Erratic school grades
- Skipping school
- Extra-curricular activities dropped
- Family activities avoided
- Refusal to do chores
- Change in family communication
- Unpredictable mood swints
- Conning behavior
- Feelings of depression expressed
- Frequent sore throats, red eyes, cough
- Minor delinquent involvement
- No savings from an after-school job
- Unexplained phone calls/visits from unfamiliar people

Stage 3: **PREOCCUPATION WITH THE MOOD SWING/HARMFUL DEPENDENCE**

- School failure (more frequent skipping classes)
- Vocal disrespect shown teachers in classroom
- Amotivational behavior
- Pathalogical lying
- Rebellious dress styles (influenced by drug culture)
- Police incidents: DWI's, stealing/shoplifting
- Money or valuables missing from home
- Diluted or missing liquor supply at home
- "Straight" friends dropped . . . companions now are losers.

Stage 4: **USING DRUGS/DRINK JUST TO FEEL NORMAL**

- Complete rejection of family values
- Paranoia; violent anger and aggression
- Physical deterioration: Weight loss, chronic cough
- Repeated drug busts and jail sentences
- No friends

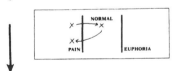

INSANITY OR DEATH

By: William C. Van Ost, M.D., F.A.A.P., Founder & Director
The Van Ost Institute for Family Living, Englewood, NJ

9

TWELVE STEPS

THE DIRECTION IS UP

"Driven to drink," as Charles Deutsch writes in *Broken Bottles, Broken Dreams*, "is an idiom imbedded in our language like a bad debt passed on through the generations." It is, in fact, a misconception. No one can drive another person to drink. It is the mother, the father, the youngster, who open their *own* mouths, following their *own* convictions that relief is just a swallow or toke away. But while addiction is no one's fault, just as diabetes is no one's fault, the addict does "own" his disease, in just the same sense that a diabetic does. Neither the addiction nor the diabetes belong to anyone else.

Once someone is in trouble with a chemical, that person has to come to terms with his or her own denial ("I can handle it"). And no treatment can work until the person who's sick says "I need help." This does not mean, however, that you should wait to get help for your child until she's ready to "own" her addiction. Kids who are chemical dependents need treatment right away, and it's up to adults to find it for them, even if it means forcing them into it. With rare exception, adolescents are not self-motivated to seek treatment, and will seldom ask for help on their own—somebody has to force the issue. Of course, however much the kid may kick and scream at first, he or she eventually will have to be able to say, "Okay, this is *my* problem—*I* have it, and *I* have to be responsible for doing something about it."

Our experience with chemical dependency affords us some strongly held beliefs. One of the most important of them is that the kind of treatment that works best for kids—or anyone, for that matter—who are hooked is one that is based on the tenets of Alcoholics Anonymous. AA, with over ten million members worldwide, has had an enormous impact on our society. Its Twelve Steps have been directly adopted by Al-Anon and Alateen, for members of the alcoholic's family, as well as by Families Anonymous, Adult Children of Alcoholics, Narcotics Anonymous, Gamblers Anonymous, Overeaters Anonymous, and other self-help groups. If the 1970's were the decade of the "me" generation, the 1980's have been the decade of addictions—not just to alcohol and drugs, but to food, sex, relationships, and work.

AA is there for people who all said, at one point in their lives, "I can handle it." The AA rejoinder to that is "No, you can't." AA enables alcoholics to achieve sobriety by admitting their powerlessness over alcohol. The first three of the Twelve Steps, which are at the core of the program, relate to the admission of personal defeat.

1. We admitted we were powerless over alcohol—that our lives had become unmanageable.
2. Came to believe that a Power greater than ourselves could restore us to sanity.
3. Made a decision to turn our will and our lives over to the care of God, *as we understood Him.*

Steps four through nine deal with repairing the past.

4. Made a searching and fearless moral inventory of ourselves.
5. Admitted to God, to ourselves, and to another human being the exact nature of our wrongs.
6. Were entirely ready to have God remove all these defects of character.
7. Humbly asked Him to remove our shortcomings.
8. Made a list of all persons we had harmed, and became willing to make amends to them all.
9. Made direct amends to such people wherever possible, except when to do so would injure them or others.

And the last three focus on maintaining a sense of peace and calm in the daily living of the present, putting an end to the preoccupation with alcohol.

10. Continued to take personal inventory and when we were wrong promptly admitted it.
11. Sought through prayer and meditation to improve our conscious contact with God, *as we understood Him,* praying only for knowledge of His will for us and the power to carry that out.
12. Having had a spiritual awakening as the result of these steps, we tried to carry this message to alcoholics and to practice these principles in all our affairs.

These steps, reprinted in Appendix 4, serve as spiritual guidelines, closely related to the well-known AA serenity prayer: "God grant me the serenity to accept the things I cannot change, the courage to change the things I can, and the wisdom to know the difference."

Before coming to AA, or any of the "Anonymous" groups, *most* drug abusers are sure that if they just change the way they think, or act differently, they'll be able to control their addiction—not realizing that *the task of recovery is to discover a whole other way of being that is not based on willpower.* Ending the pretense of being in control, of being powerful, is essential for what AA calls a spiritual awakening. (AA makes a clear distinction between religion, with its attendant dogma, and spirituality, which requires no more than a provisional belief in any power greater than oneself.)

Many traditional psychotherapists and psychiatrists, failing to understand why conventional therapy is not enough to resolve serious addiction problems, eventually dismiss the alcoholic addict, and/or his or her family, as "unmotivated."

AA generates what one family expert has called "a planned spontaneous remission." One does not know when it will occur, but one knows that it *will* occur if the drinker participates in the AA program. In the early days, many people got sober in AA only after hitting a "low bottom"—losing their health, their families, their jobs.

Today, thanks to the evolution of the program, and the techniques of early intervention, problem drinkers can have a "high bottom": The alcoholic is brought face to face with the present and future consequences of the drinking without having to have her life fall apart.

Because she can see where the path of her drinking is taking her, she doesn't have to go down it.

If you are the parent of a youngster whose present drug use worries you, you may be saying, "Okay, yes, I see that AA might be the saving of an *adult* alcoholic, but my kid—stubborn, angry, resentful, denying, and mutinous about any parental suggestions—would never go along with that." Not at first, perhaps, but you simply have to take our word for it: The best, the most successful, adolescent treatment centers in the country are modeled on the precepts of Alcoholics Anonymous.

A FAMILY AFFAIR

What it is crucial to understand is that no AA program is going to work well for an adolescent without the total commitment and involvement of the family in his treatment. While he or she is at a treatment center, and afterward, too, the other members of the family must participate in the recovery—because the family as a whole has been just as deeply affected as the addict/alcoholic.

All of AA's principles apply equally to family members—they too are powerless over the disease, their lives as well have become unmanageable. Recognizing the need to involve the family, Al-Anon, Nar-Anon, Alateen, Families Anonymous, and other Twelve-Step programs arose to meet that need.

"I'm not the one who has the problem" won't work. "We all have the problem, and we can all get better" *will* work. You will hear members of self-help groups referring to their organization as "the program" or "the fellowship." What are the questions most commonly asked about these programs?

- *How do I find a meeting?*
  Look in your phone book and call. You will not be asked to give your name—you will simply be given the location and time of meetings near you.
- *Where are the meetings?*
  They can be anywhere—churchs, hospitals, treatment centers, spare office rooms, in almost any town in this country and in most countries throughout the world.
- *How often do they meet?*
  Each group meets weekly at the same time and place, every week of the year. On any given day there are several meetings available. There may be fewer meetings in smaller towns.
- *What do you mean by anonymity?*
  First names only are used at meetings and privacy is inviolate.
- *What if I see a neighbor there?*
  They are there for the same reason you are, and value their own anonymity as much as you do yours.
- *How can I join?*
  You just go to the meeting. There are no dues or fees, but voluntary donations pay the rent, pay for the literature and the coffee, etc.
- *How long do I have to go?*
  That's up to you—there are no rules regarding attendance. It's your personal choice.
- *What if they ask me to talk?*
  Do what's comfortable for you—if you only want to listen, that's okay. But remember that what's said at meetings stays there.

• *What does "having a sponsor" mean?*
A sponsor is someone who has been through the ropes before you, who can help you by listening and, gently but firmly, guiding you—through example and by sharing personal stories. A good sponsor will not give advice or direction, but will be there for you when you are in need.

All of these Twelve-Step programs were founded on the principle that people who have common problems benefit from joining together to share their experiences, strength, and hope.

Chemical dependency is a family disease. These fellowships offer support for each affected member. As millions of people have discovered, these programs work.

10

PROFESSIONAL HELP

HOW TO SHOP FOR THE BEST
Chapter Revision by William Carlos, Jr.
Executive Director, The Van Ost Institute for Family Living, Inc.,

Later in this chapter we'll tell you exactly how to go
about finding the help you need, but let's talk first about
what you'll be looking for. Most obviously, it's this: You
want someone who can either confirm or deny your own
suspicions that you've got a youngster with an alcohol or
other drug problem. Someone who can assess the degree of
trouble involved; who can be relied on to discover
whether it's abuse or addiction; and who'll then
recommend the best course of action for you to take.

When we say "professional help," we don't necessarily mean people with medical degrees but, more
accurately, people who have training specifically in the
treatment of chemical dependency. *That's* what you are
going to be looking for: a person, or persons, *experienced in
working with and treating the disease of addiction.*

It might be helpful at this point for you to understand
how The Van Ost Institute For Family Living functions, as
it is representative of the kind of place that we are
suggesting that you should try to find. What makes it
this way is the result of the professional training and
backgrounds of its counselors which has given them both
the knowledge and the ability to use an oft-proven

holistic approach to treatment; resulting in the patient receiving the benefit of a caring, supportive environment in which to begin the recovery process. Members of a properly credentialed and/or licensed clinical staff are able to recognize chemical dependency as a treatable illness which is adversely affecting its victims who are deserving of empathic, professional care. A team of counselors trained in this approach holds out much needed help and hope for those who are willing to enter treatment.

Because the Institute's staff knows that addiction is a family disease and that everyone in the family is affected by one member's illness, it provides the tools that enable each individual to break through the family denial and deal with the facts. As professionals, they know that families that get sick together can get well together, if strict attention is paid to all of its member's concerns, helping each to nurture self-esteem while giving love and support to the one seeking recovery.

The Institute is modeled after other successful programs across the country; dynamic programs which we know work; that are based on the concepts of the twelve step, self-help groups. It's staff continues to research new and innovative intervention strategies that address the special needs of an addicted family. One such strategy that is working successfully for the Institute's adolescent population is a resiliency approach to treatment which focuses on the young person's own strengths as well as the internal and external assets that the family, community and the school can bring together to address the challenges of adolescent addiction.

The Van Ost Institute, is a nonprofit, private, outpatient facility with inpatient affiliations carefully selected to provide higher levels of care as deemed necessary by its professional staff. A combination of professional services, plus ongoing support offered by the Twelve-Step groups, the Institute's own unique Mentoring Program and other available support systems provide the tools needed to smooth the path to full recovery for each family member. The professional services offered by the Institute are as follows:

1. An Initial Intake, For Assessment and Diagnosis.

During an extensive intake interview, the extent of the problem is determined, whether it's abuse or addiction, and then suggestions are made for what can be done. The complete procedure ideally involves all appropriate family members. It covers chemical abuse and it effects on everyone. It includes an in-depth family history that deals with everyone's background. If it is felt to be necessary, special medical consultation or other referrals may be arranged.

Adolescents are referred to the Institute in varying stages of disease progression. Thus, a key finding of a good assessment is the determination of the level of the adolescent's involvement with addictive chemicals, whether the problem is one of abuse or actual addiction, in order to provide the professional staff with the necessary information to develop an appropriate individualized treatment plan. For those whose use has become chronic or is escalating; and/or if medical complications are compromising their health, a residential program may be urged in order to stabilize the situation. In this stage of the disease, it is the rare adolescent who will cooperate and willingly accept treatment. If the addicted person is a minor under age 18, you have the right legally and morally, to force the issue. *It is not his or her choice-- A life is at stake.*

2. Intervention.
This involves the interruption of the drug-using behavior pattern on the part of the adolescent as well as the enabling attitudes of his or her family and friends.

It may be accomplished during the initial intake; and it usually is in the case of an adolescent. The level of chemical involvement may result in immediate referral to an inpatient treatment facility. While there are still many treatment centers throughout the country, we suggest that you choose only those facilities which have a proven treatment success rate with adolescent patients.

We prefer centers that have effective programs that address the physical, social, psychological, and family issues, vital components of good treatment and recovery.

Sometimes, however, the picture is not clear. The counselor may not be sure of the extent of the problem. The patient may be in such an early stage of usage that inpatient treatment would be premature. Then an alternate treatment can be arranged which would involve outpatient counseling with strict chemical testing. In such cases the adolescent is asked to agree to the monitoring. At that time, the patient will be told that entrance to a preselected inpatient rehabilitation program will be required if he or she is unable to stay "clean and dry."

3. Counseling and Therapy. Where chemical dependency is concerned, every one seeking treatment feels that he or she is special and as such must receive individual therapy. In fact, what we know about the nature of this illness is that treatment for most individuals who are being adversely affected by living in a home where there is an alcohol or drug addicted family member will achieve much better therapeutic results if counseled in a group setting.

People who are addicted tend to see themselves as unique----they frequently are fearful of sharing their inner feelings with others. Years of living with the "family secret" has reinforced this belief. A group helps people learn to trust others, and move on to a healthy recovery.

Of course, individual and family counseling can be therapeutically indicated. The decision about which treatment approach should be followed in order to provide the most effective results is best made with the advice of a competent professional staff member of a well-run treatment facility.

4. Co-Dependency Counseling Services. These are offered to family and friends of the chemically addicted individual, whether or not that person is in recovery. It would be ideal if all addiction   treatment facilities would provide special co-dependency treatment groups for the non-addicted family members: the younger children, adolescents, parents, seniors and the adult children of addicted parents. Our Institute, thanks in part to   the financial help of many generous donors, offers each of the services. "A family which gets sick together needs to get well together."

A socially conscious treatment center should offer more to the community than just clinical services. For nearly two decades, we have provided continuing education programs to professional groups as well as free educational lectures, forums and awareness programs to various audiences such as service clubs, seniors groups, hospitals, schools, houses of worship, and the media.

Many other centers offer similar services. Now, we will show you how to find them:

JUST A PHONE
CALL AWAY

Here are several ways to pursue a line of inquiry that may guide you to treatment centers in your area:

*Get out the yellow pages of your local phone book.
If you live in a small town, get the yellow pages of the nearest large city. Look under "Alcoholism Information and Treatment Centers." (Remember that alcoholism and drug addiction are interchangeable in this context.) You'll find listings like these, which we found in the yellow pages of a randomly selected, good-sized town in New Jersey:

- Alcohol Abuse and Intervention Service
- Alcoholism Advisory Service—24-hour hotline
- Alcoholism Counseling
- Drug-Counseling Service
- Family Center for Alcohol and Drug Counseling

In addition to these listings, we found advertisements for eleven different treatment centers and hospital help programs offering alcohol and drug treatment, intervention services, and so on. There are literally hundreds and hundreds of treatment centers in this country.

Here are some other sources of information:

- Attend an open meeting of Alcoholics or Narcotics Anonymous in your area. (Your phone book will give you the number to call.) Ask when "open meetings" are held and where ("open" means nonalcoholics/addicts are welcome to attend). Talk to an A.A. or N.A. member and ask if anyone in the group can recommend a good treatment center. People will be eager to help you—and word-of-mouth is an excellent way to discover the best. Do the same with Al-Anon or Nar-Anon.
- Call the National Council on Alcoholism (there are regional branches of the organization) and ask them to recommend a treatment center.
- Go to your local library and ask for periodicals and journals that list alcohol and drug treatment centers.
- If the teachers or counselors in your local school have had training in addiction, ask them about treatment programs.
- If your doctor understands alcohol and drug use, ask her.

As you conduct your search, it's important to remember that, if your child is in trouble with chemicals, he can't be effectively treated *until he is off of them.* A "slip" is sometimes a part of recovery, but relapse involving continued use should be neither expected or accepted. Too many parents would rather that their youngster's problem be identified as due to some "underlying psychopathological illness" rather than the straightforward DSM IV diagnosis of alcohol or drug abuse or addiction. And, sadly, there are still far too many psychiatrists and psychotherapists who do not demand abstinence as a condition of treatment.

If your youngster is in therapy now, and getting better, then fine--we want you to do whatever works with your youngster. But if he or she is still drinking or taking drugs while in treatment, then the therapist is *talking to the chemical,* not your child. *Unless and until chemical dependency is treated as the primary problem, there is little chance that your child is going to get better.*

One therapist that we know of accepts chemically dependent kids for individual therapy and allows them to continue drinking and drugging. When he invariably fails in his quest to get them to "cut down," let alone stop using at all, he sends them on their way with some AA literature. We know of this malpractice as he has twice asked us for more AA material!

Once you've located some treatment centers in your area, call them...better yet, visit their facilities and become sure that they offer programs that will fit your child's needs.

CHOOSING A TREATMENT CENTER

In judging a residential center's effectiveness, there are three elements of its operation that we consider essential:

1. Its program must be centered on the A.A. Twelve-Step approach to recovery. This is important not only for the reasons we gave in Chapter Nine, but also because such a center will have on staff a good mix of recovering alcoholics, and others affected by the illness. These people will know from experience what your child is going through and how best to handle him or her with empathetic concern, but also with the right degree of toughness, when it's called for.

2. The program must be strongly family oriented. This means not just that you'll be allowed to see your child for an hour on weekends or visiting days, but that the center conducts a program involving all members of the family, preferably one with an entire five- to seven-day family week. The right treatment center will be dedicated to the proposition that progression of the disease can be arrested, and family life restored to normal, in an atmosphere of honesty, love, and hope for the future. Here's a fact proved over and over again: Addiction is the only chronic, progressive disease in which everyone affected by it is, after recovery, better than they were before they got sick!

3. The program must be accredited by the Joint Commission on Accrediting Hospitals, thus assuring professional care for your child.

In the next chapter we'll tell you exactly what your kid will be going through in the treatment center you take him to. But for now let's just say that you won't be abandoning your youngster, as some parents fear, to a kind of adult prison in which mental patients are mistreated by bullying aides. While there is a natural parental tendency to regard putting youngsters into treatment as a harsh measure, sometimes this is the only choice you have.

We recently ran into a lawyer friend who confessed to being upset over the fact that his son, a junior in high school, had had a diagnostic work-up (not done by us) that resulted in the recommendation of a treatment center for the boy. "Don't you think that's a pretty *radical* decision?" the lawyer asked. What Bill said to him in reply was, "After my heart attack a few years ago, I could have died from the radical decision I made to let surgeons open up my chest and lift the heart out to perform a bypass operation. That 'radical' decision *saved my life*." The friend saw Bill's point. It hadn't occurred to him that far from feeling imprisoned, his son would discover that, in an attractive and comfortable setting, he could get more hugs every day than perhaps he's ever had.

Paying the Price

There is something you should know right up front about treatment centers—they are costly. Some final bills will come to several thousand dollars. Your medical insurance policy is likely to cover a good part of it, but still . . .

What we tell parents is this: How can you put a price on a young person's life? How much has he or she *already* cost you in terms of wrecked cars, therapy that didn't work, troubles with the police? Think also of the emotional costs the kid has exacted, the toll that your worry has taken. Can you afford the *further* costs there'll be if you fail to do something about treatment *now*?

YOU'VE CHOSEN A
CENTER . . . NOW WHAT?

First off, it is important to let the treatment center know if you plan to use your insurance to cover the costs of treatment. The center that will be doing the evaluation must know the insurance company's policies regarding the level of care they will be willing to cover. It is not uncommon for them to insist that the least restrictive level of care must be tried first, prior to allowing an inpatient placement. After much experience, in these difficult times, trying to convince managed care firms that they should clear an adolescent for residential treatment, we found it very important that parents carefully document, as accurately as possible, the addictive behaviors and attitudes that were being manifested prior to the assessment.

What if your kid refuses to go?.....Tell your child that there are *no* options. No ifs, no buts.. *you're going*! If it's going to be hard for you to work up the courage to give this order, ask the treatment center to *lend* you some courage---get ideas from them on how to best handle the situation.

One way we've counseled parents on how to tell their child is by saying, "Look, we're just going for an evaluation---maybe they will tell us that you *don't* have a problem. Let's just find out for sure." A reluctant youngster who does indeed have a problem, generally agrees to go along; figuring, as he has always done before, that he can con his way through the experience. What he doesn't know is that a trained professional is hard to fool---experts are very good at cutting through a kid's claims that there's is no need for treatment...that there's no problem. No matter how angry, scared or hurt they may be when faced with the diagnosis of addiction, most will go along as, deep down , there is almost always a buried cry for help.

Don't forget one more weapon you've got: the clout of a parent. You've got the power to take something away, something that a kid wants. What? Use of the car? Going out on weekends? A part-time job? Parties? You name it, and you can remove the privilege. A holdout will knuckle under here and agree to go.

A CASE IN POINT

Not long ago we conducted a double intervention with two kids from the same family.

At the first meeting, the mother, a successful New York City department store executive, came to us to ask about help for her son, 18-year-old Matthew, whom she described as "a brilliant musician that the country's preeminent music school is dying to get." Her reason for coming to see us was her "niggling worry" that Matt *might* develop a drug problem that would inhibit the development of "a virtuoso career." We learned that the father, who'd been too busy to come along, was one of New York's most successful stock brokers. The couple had one other child, Roxanne, 17. A full-time house-keeper had been with them sixteen years because, according to the mother, "We didn't want our kids to be latchkey children." The family home was in an affluent suburb and there was a summer home, too, on Cape Cod ("not far from the Kennedy compound in Hyannisport"). Both Matthew and Roxanne owned their own cars and had their own bank accounts and, their mother told us, both had lots of friends.

Could Roxanne, we asked, also have a drug prob-lem? "Oh, no, definitely not," her mother said. But a little further casual questioning led to the discovery that Roxanne had spent some of her Christmas money, when she was 13, on a case of imported champagne for a party with her friends. "Nothing but the best for Roxy," her mother said with an amused smile.

At the second session we insisted that the father come along too. We split into groups, Bill doing an intake interview with Matthew, Elaine talking with Roxanne, and one of our staff counselors with the parents.

An hour or so later, after a discreet signal from Bill, we three counselors convened in a separate room to compare notes on what we'd learned.

Both kids were terrific con artists. Matthew, though he had a certain superficial charm, also had an ego inflated to grandiose proportions, to mask the fact, we suspected, that his "brilliance" was only skin-deep and that the music school might not share his mother's assessment of virtuosity. He was affable and cooperative throughout the interview, and he reported that he'd tried about every drug on the market (at 13, his sister remembered, he planted and tended his own pot garden on the roof of the house). Well, yes, he told Bill, it was possible that he'd wrecked his first car because he got drunk at a party. He had escaped uninjured; his girl-friend had a broken leg, "but she was okay about it." And yes, there was a DWI charge just three months later, incurred while at the wheel of his second car. These days he said that he was "only using coke now and then." It was true that his grades were "pretty terrible" last term, but he was going to pull himself together *this* term because the music school "might be a pain in the ass about it."

Roxy was your basic teeny-bopper, also cooperative and chatty, happy to talk about Matthew's problems ("He does coke just about every day"), her mother's problems, her father's problems. She was very good at the victim role: Her mother didn't understand her and was always mad at her for no reason at all, she said, her father never paid any attention to her, and the house-keeper had a "mean streak." As for herself, yes, sure, she'd tried pot and liquor and even coke, just once, when Matt gave her some. But "I'm not really into that stuff," she said. (What we learned from Matthew, who'd been dealing since he was 14, was that Roxy's champagne party at 13 had included cocaine for her guests—and he was still keeping her supplied on a weekly basis.)

Matthew and Roxanne's mother, who looked to be about thirty pounds overweight, periodically went to a diet-control clinic but never succeeded in losing more than a token two or three pounds. The father spent little time at home; a heavy drinker, he had a charge account at the neighborhood's finest bar.

The family picture reflected tension and unhap-piness—in other words, extreme dysfunction. The good things money can buy had hardly produced a happy family.

After our consultation, we re-grouped. We told the parents exactly what we'd learned about the two kids, and gave our collective counselor opinion that *both* Matt and Roxy needed to be in treatment centers. Roxy began howling immediately: "I can't believe you *did* this to me! *I'm* not the one with a problem, *he* is!" And Matt immediately started bargaining: "Look, you don't understand—I just don't do well in group situations like I know they have. I'll see a therapist here if you want me to, okay? But I just can't take the idea of going away—it just wouldn't *work* for me!"

Both parents were in shock. As it wore off, they each gave us their own version of the "not-my-kid" routine. When we suggested a treatment center in the West (we felt that with this particular family it was best to put some distance between the kids and their parents), the mother suddenly turned maternal and protested, "But they'll be so far *away*—there must be better places nearby!" The father angrily declared that he didn't see "why the hell we have to be so drastic about this!"

Once again we went quietly over the painful truth. Matt and Roxy were both in late-stage addiction. Without in-patient treatment, they would not find their way back to health. Without help, the prognosis for recovery was dismal. To hammer home the points we made, we spoke aloud the last fearful truth: The kids were addicted, and they could die from their addiction.

Two days later, both brother and sister were on their way west to treatment. Their parents had heard us.

The treatment took. Both kids have been drug-free for over a year now, and all four members of the family still come for counseling on a regular basis.

We confess we'd never have bet on it—it couldn't have happened to a more difficult family. Now, let's get back to yours.

11

WHAT GOES ON IN
A TREATMENT CENTER?

HOW TO GET YOUR KID BACK

Some look like resorts. Or health spas, or country estates, or small college campuses. They may sit snugly within the seclusion of pine woods, or hug the shoreline of a lake, or be spread across rolling green hill country. Everything about them invites the eye and suggests tranquil order within.

These are treatment centers; nothing about them hints at detention—or even "treatment," for that matter. They are also known colloquially as "rehabs," and indeed, rehabilitation is their mission. Some centers take both adolescents and adults, others minister just to kids, or just to adults.

For the adult population, the term rehab is apt: The process of treatment is a form of re-education. A chemical dependent, suddenly separated from the drug, will be shaky and uncertain at first, but he will be handed the tools he needs to help change the life he was leading (and losing). It has been some time, after all, since he's acted as an alert and responsible member of society, and he has much to re-learn about the way the world works when one is not backing away from its realities with drugs or alcohol. In a rehab, he learns how to go about restructuring himself—how he must adjust his thinking, and alter his behavior, and, yes, search as well for the restoration of his spirit.

When he leaves the rehab, he is opting for a life that holds the promise of a new and better way of *being* in the world: a life of conscious sobriety.

With kids, it's different. In terms of their recovery, the rehabs ought to be called "habilitation" centers, because kids get themselves into trouble at an age when they haven't yet had the time it takes to develop coping mechanisms—unlike adults, they don't have years of living experience to fall back on. And that makes it very tough for them: They can't re-learn, or re-structure, or re-store a life that had barely begun before it got knocked for a loop.

Much of the important work of growing up is done in early adolescence. The tough stuff that a kid normally has to go through and learn how to handle, through these roller-coaster years, is blotted out for the addicted adolescent. This child hasn't learned how to handle things like the pain of a friend's rejection, or the anxiety of dealing with a body that is changing, or how to adjust to the rules that society demands for her. A treatment center has to "habilitate" kids more or less from scratch.

If you want your kid to recover, here's what you have to do to get him back in a stage of recovery: Trust a good treatment center. Do what they tell you to do.

THE FIRST DAYS ARE
THE HARDEST

The day you finally get your child to a treatment center and leave her there, you'll probably return home exhausted, as well as relieved to have your teenager in someone else's hands—for now, at any rate.

It's been an emotional seesaw for everyone involved. And it's going to go on being just that way for a good deal longer.

At first, your kid may call (what kid would write when he or she can phone collect?) and you'll hear it *all*. The first time, perhaps, it will be a tearful shriek: "Get me *out of here*, I can't *stand* it, they're all just a bunch of *druggies!*" (When, for example, her own problem is alcohol). Then another time: "Listen, there's this really neat counselor, Mom, he's an alcoholic himself and he says he's sure I'll make out okay, but he says I have to get my sea legs here, whatever that is, and I'm feeling a lot better . . ." And yet another time, between sobs: "They're just playing *games* with me, Daddy, they can't really make things okay and I know they can't, and I just want you and Mom to come and get me . . ."

So what's going on there—what *is* it they're putting the poor kid through?

First a description of who "they" are: some of the best treatment centers work—with a staff team of physicians, psychologists, nurses, social workers, and family therapists who've all been professionally trained in chemical dependency. Many of the health professionals are likely to be recovering from the disease themselves. (Since AA recognizes that the illness is one that afflicts its victims throughout their lifetimes, just as diabetics continue to be diabetics, its members often speak of themselves as "recovering alcoholics," seldom "recovered.")

The program of a typical adolescent center, in which the length of stay for primary treatment averages six to eight weeks, will basically work like this:

When the patient arrives, he will be greeted warmly—often with a hug—but will soon discover that things are different then they were at home. Since so many kids try to bring in at least a modicum of drugs (remember that their need is overpowering and the prospect of being out of touch with a supplier can be terrifying), the new patient will be searched, and his baggage will be carefully examined, piece by piece, for hidden drugs. Alternately, some kids welcome disciplined treatment, knowing, if not acknowledging, that it's what they've needed all along.

Next, a complete physical assessment will be made, including lab tests. Any medical complications resulting from chemical use will be promptly treated. Patients will be kept under careful nurse and doctor surveillance for the first few days to monitor possible problems in detoxification. Also during the first few days, the process of testing and psycho-social evaluation will begin. From the outset, the patient will be participating in a tightly scheduled daily program. It will consist of group-counseling to help a kid identify with his addiction—to overcome denial, minimizing, and the conning behavior that has become a way of life for him. The addicted adolescent will have to realize that he is experiencing only the first steps in a recovery process.

A good treatment center knows how tough these

first few days and weeks are, and supplements group sessions with individual attention. However, the group process remains the foundation for solid recovery. After all, this youngster isolated herself and her feelings from most of the community. She sees herself as alone and unique, no matter how gregarious she may have seemed to her friends. So interacting with her peers in a group gives her the tools to reenter society as a functioning, healthy member.

INTERMEDIATE CARE

Now the youngster will settle into a daily routine— although dealing with adolescents is *never* a predictable routine.

There will be a structured daily program for the duration of the patient's stay: Community meetings, group therapy, individual counseling, lectures, and attendance at Twelve-Step meetings will be part of the regimen.

Here's how a typical day might break down:

7–7:30	Rise, dress, tidy room
7:30–8	Breakfast
8–8:30	Daily medical checkup
8:30–9	Individual counseling or "personal" time
9–9:45	Lecture
10–11:15	Group therapy
11:30–12	Reading group
12–1	Lunch and open time
1–1:45	Lecture
1:45–2:45	Group therapy session

3–3:45	Exercise time
4–5	Community group
5–6	Dinner
6:15–7	Lecture
7:30–8:30	AA, NA, or Al-Anon speaker's meeting
8:30–10:30	Study or open time
10:30	Lights out

A pretty tight schedule, isn't it? It's planned that way, because for the addicted adolescent, "free" time was always "trouble" time. This may be your child's first experience of a disciplined daily routine. The confines of this schedule, or one like it, begin to restore (or introduce) predictability and planning in the youngster's life.

THE FOUR STAGES OF RECOVERY

It's well known that *all* patients in treatment go through several stages of emotional development as they recover. Vernon Johnson described these stages in his excellent book *I'll Quit Tomorrow* (Harper and Row). We want to tell you briefly about them, to help you understand why a patient's moods and reactions are different from week to week, something that often creates consternation on the part of parents (or, in the case of adults, the family).

The stages of recovery are of varying length and intensity, and time is loosely described, because sometimes they don't all happen in treatment but may occur later.

The first but toughest stage of recovery during treatment is *admission* that there is a problem with a chemical. This is when a person can truthfully say, "I

belong here." The second stage, *compliance*, is characterized by the patient's need to figure out what it is that
these counselors want: "Just tell me what it is and I'll do
it for you." Compliance can make things look as though
they're great, but often the old con mechanism is at
work here: They attempt to fool themselves and those
around them into believing they're happy to be there.
"This program is wonderful. It's just what I needed, I'm
so grateful to be here."

It may fool parents, but not the professional. The
third stage, that of *acceptance*, signals an increased self-
awareness of the serious nature of the illness: "I was so
sick." A patient begins to know, on a gut level, that he
really is addicted. Donning rose-tinted glasses, these
people declare, "I'll never be like *that* again." Finally,
surrender occurs when a person develops an honest
awareness that he has absolutely no control over his
addiction. He's not a little god of any kind, he is truly
powerless. He now knows that it's quite possible that, as
much as he wants to get better, he may fail to do so. He
has been given the tools for recovery and his job is to
pick them up and use them. What he's learned in
treatment is that it's the only way.

FAMILY CARE

We believe that the best treatment programs involve a
commitment by the entire family to recovery for themselves as well as for their addicted family member.
Because of their own feelings of desperation, some
parents admit their kid to a treatment facility, expecting
it to fix him up and send him back all cured, just the way

he was before he started using drugs. It doesn't happen that way. This is a family disease; everyone is affected.

The best family programs include a five-day residential program for family members as a vital component of recovery. Family week generally is scheduled in the latter part of in-patient treatment. In this sort of program, the family, like the patient, learn about the disease, experience group process, and are encouraged to commit to a continuing recovery program.

A child who returns to a home in which family members are not in any ongoing recovery program themselves has a much smaller chance of staying sober and straight. We can't stress this enough: To leave a teenager to do his or her "own thing" toward recovery is like sticking a Band-Aid over a gunshot wound. It isn't good enough.

CONTINUING CARE (AFTERCARE)

Plans are made while the patient is still in treatment for what will become his regimen following discharge. Similar plans are also formulated for each member near the conclusion of their family week.

The goal of continuing care is to consolidate the gains made during in-patient treatment by both the patient and the family. It's like having a road map for continuing recovery—a plan for shaping a satisfying way of life.

For both the patient and her family, aftercare may consist of a combination of professional help, support groups, individual treatment, family therapy, and commitment to the appropriate self-help groups such as AA,

Al-Anon, and others. AA contacts and other arrangements for aftercare treatment are often initiated by the in-patient center before the person goes home.

Many adolescents need far longer therapy than is provided by primary treatment. A good center, recognizing this, will refer those youngsters to halfway houses, which can ease the transition back to the general community. If a halfway house is suggested, support the decision. So many kids desperately need additional time in a protected environment.

A Note of Warning

If either parent is a user or abuser of chemicals, continuation of that process when the child returns home can sabotage his treatment. Good centers will make concerted efforts to intervene in that parent's own addiction.

This can happen early in the course of treatment or during the family sessions. In fact, some centers will not accept the child of an actively using parent who will be actually living with the family.

If the parent refuses to look at his own problem, the child's chances of staying clean and sober can be seriously jeopardized.

Whatever happens, it's going to be a profound learning experience for all. Have faith. It works.

12

THE WORST THAT

COULD HAPPEN

IS YOUR CHILD SUICIDAL?

If you picked up your newspaper and saw that a 747, carrying a planeload of over 400 adolescents, had crashed and everyone on board was killed, you'd be horrified, wouldn't you? What if other such planeloads of kids crashed each month this year—with the same loss of life? That would amount to a senseless death for over 6,000 kids in a year. Wouldn't there be a national hysterical demand for action in the matter?

That's how many of this country's kids die by their own hand each year. Eighteen kids a day, every day, commit suicide. Another 250,000 to 500,000 of them attempt it.

Actually, many authorities think these rates are considerably understated. Officials avoid classifying deaths as suicide if it's possible to do so, for many reasons—because of the traumatic impact a suicide has on those who are left behind, because of exclusionary clauses in insurance policies, or even because of legal reasons, since in some states a death can't be classified as suicide unless a note is found. The real incidence of suicide has been estimated to be as much as three times that which is reported.

In any event, there are some scary statistical certainties: since 1950, the rate of suicide for those between the ages of 15 and 24 has increased 300%—and the rate is climbing at three times the rate for the general population. This is an epidemic! Why?

We think one of the main reasons for the increase is drug abuse. These figures on suicide closely parallel the increasing use of alcohol and drugs by teenagers. An estimated 35% of the kids who kill themselves are known substance abusers. In the non-abuser balance of 65%, chemical dependency is frequently a problem *elsewhere in the family.*

Medical examiners report the presence of alcohol in the bodies of a large percentage of suicides. The suicide rate for alcoholics is 50 times higher than that of the population at large—bearing out Karl Menninger's view that chemical dependency is *a chronic form of suicide.*

Who are these suicidal youngsters? Why are they brought to the brink of such despair? And what warning signs should parents be on the look-out for? Here are some answers.

WHO

A recent study done by researchers at Washington University School of Medicine in St. Louis determined several specific factors involved in suicide of the young. The study was conducted with 3,000 kids between the ages of 13 and 18 who came to free clinics for medical care in ten major cities, including Boston, Los Angeles, and New Orleans.

In addition to the expected findings that adolescents who use drugs were the ones most likely to attempt suicide, researchers found that depression often coexisted with aberrant behavior—stealing, truancy, vandalism, prostitution, and so on.

Running away from home was striking in its association with suicide attempts. Of those who had run away, 24 percent had tried suicide. Over a third of the group who had run away as often as three times had attempted it. Why did they run away in the first place?

One might think that suicide among the young is more an urban than a rural phenomenon, yet a recent study of 7,000 high-school students in rural Minnesota found that suicide-attempt rates were five to six times *greater* there than rates previously described by other investigators looking at other populations. Over a six-month period, the prevalence of suicide attempts was a startling seven percent!

In a study of 48 California teenagers who killed themselves during the first third of 1986 and then underwent "psychological autopsies," half of the kids, according to the Los Angeles Suicide Prevention Center, were classified as depressed/withdrawn, and a third as aggressive/impulsive. The aggressive/impulsive kids had had lots of problems with substance abuse, fighting, and other destructive behaviors. The seemingly normal were high achievers under stress; they had thought of themselves as imposters hiding personal defects. Half of the entire group had been under the influence of drugs and/or had alcohol at the time of death. (A question not addressed was how many of those youngsters came from alcoholic households.)

In another study, of 79 California kids who reported having suicidal thoughts and discussing the matter with someone, 69 of them had told a friend. But only one had told her parents. Indeed, parental pressures and problems at home were among the reasons the majority of this group said they had felt like killing themselves. Clearly, parents absorbed in their own lives and careers can provoke feelings of alienation and rejection in their youngsters—feelings that can lead to suicide attempts.

WHY

Mental-health practitioners attribute the increasing rate of teen suicide to many causes: faster-paced lives, the decline of organized religion, competitiveness at school, and the tightening of the job market.

There are also those who see a link between suicide and the playthings of the Eighties—personal computers, VCRs, MTV. Writing in the *Journal of Independent Social Work* last year, a trio of counselors had this to say: "Perhaps the move to a technocratic society and its inherent insensitivities to human emotion have caused an increased sense of hopelessness."

Others point to the changes that have been wrung on family life. For many kids, a traditional family structure no longer exists; divorce, separation, and remarriage have created new pressures. The things that used to keep people together and give kids a sense of solidity and trust in the future simply aren't there anymore. Young people, seeing that their hard-driving parents are unhappy despite their achievements, may decide that their own future holds little hope for them, and the sense of pessimism that develops is far more pervasive than it's ever been in past generations.

This same kind of hopelessness and helplessness is an inherent part of living in today's conflict-ridden world, threatened always by nuclear disaster. Against this background, some young people simply aren't taking setbacks as well as previous generations did, and suicide seems to be the last step in an accelerated process of breakdown.

HOW

Often kids first try to relieve their pain and problems with alcohol. At the beginning it seems to work—they actually do feel better for a while. But the pressure builds as they experiment with drugs—and with sex—before they're able to deal with the emotional consequences of what they're doing.

The role of chemical dependency in suicide is a complex one. As we've said alcohol and drugs, which are used to relieve stress, especially by those who can't seem to handle the ordinary stresses of daily life, deprive users of control over their impulses. Kids, like adults, suffer from depression and loneliness and rejection and fear and anger. But kids, unlike adults, don't have the life experience behind them that would make them realize that the circumstances of their lives will *change*. They so often can't see beyond today, when they feel just as miserable as they did yesterday and the day before that and the day before that—and so tomorrow, they think, will be just as bad, and their unhappiness, it seems to them, will last forever and ever.

Another factor worth emphasizing is that adolescent suicides tend to be imitative. Kids can romanticize what they see on television or read in the papers and conclude that trying to do away with themselves would be a glamorous way to get attention. For an impulsive kid, not stopping to reckon with the permanence of death, it can be a way to "get even" with someone: "I'll die and you'll be sorry." They see themselves as the stars of their own funerals—and the reality and finality of death escape them as they "daydream" of waking up to find everyone sorry. This can create a ripple effect: a cluster of suicides that follow ones that get national attention. Suicidologists are rightly concerned with such phenomena.

As all of us know, attempts at suicide are often cries for help that too often go unheeded. How can we keep ourselves alert to hear them? Seventy percent of teenage suicide attempts are made between three P.M. and midnight, when the kids could be seen, stopped, and saved. So what do we look for?

WHAT

Here are the high-risk factors:

Drug and alcohol abuse. Which came first, the chicken or the egg? However we try to answer the question, the fact remains that 10 to 20 percent of American adolescents are problem drinkers, and when you're drunk or stoned, doing the unthinkable seems easier.

Family disruption. Marital instability, divorce, separation, or chronic discord can make a kid feel scared, unloved, rejected. Family trouble is the single problem most often cited by suicidal kids.

History of suicide in the family. A parent, a grandparent, or another close relative who's been a suicide, or who's had a history of mental disorders, is an obvious influence on a child's thinking.

A close friend who commits suicide. Forty percent of the youngsters in a Kansas study who had made suicide attempts had friends who'd killed themselves.

Unpleasant life change. A move to a new neighborhood, rejection by a close friend (usually of the opposite sex), pregnancy or a critical physical problem, remarriage of a parent, or death in the family can all contribute to suicidal feelings.

Previous suicide threat or attempt. Any child who talks of suicide must be taken seriously—*particularly* someone who's given you the idea that he or she has a specific plan (exactly how and when) and the means to carry it out (a gun, access to a car, a supply of pills, enough money to carry through plans).

Sexual abuse. One study reports that 25 percent of the girls who attempt suicide have been sexually abused. (One should not forget, of course, that boys also can be abused.) It's also worth noting that in our own experience, the vast majority of sexually abusing parents or parent figures prove to be addicted to alcohol or other drugs.

WARNING SIGNS OF THE WORST THAT COULD HAPPEN

Your observation of one or more of these red flags does not mean you have a suicidal child on your hands, of course, but because the intent of this book is to alert you to all the dangers involved in teenage chemical dependency, we feel it's important for you to stay alert to all the suicide indicators. You will find an interesting parallel in this list of indicators and the behavioral changes that occur in drug dependency (Appendix 3).

- Giving away objects of personal value (a favorite tape, a special T-shirt).
- Signs of depression: lingering sadness, tearfulness, discouragement, expressions of boredom, fatigue (sleeping a lot), hopelessness.
- Belligerent, rebellious, angry behavior.
- A drastic change in personal appearance and hygiene.
- Changes in sleep patterns: insomnia or excessive sleeping.

- Change in appetite with weight change.
- Trouble in school: dropping grades, class-skipping, problems with discipline.
- Social withdrawal: loss of friends/isolation.
- Use of alcohol and drugs.
- Preoccupation with themes of death.
- Physical complaints: stomachaches, backaches, headaches, sore throat, accidents.
- Inability to concentrate.
- Sudden interest in dangerous activities, risk-taking, impulsive behavior.
- Increased irritability, behavioral problems.
- Loss of interest in pleasure (in previously enjoyed activities).
- Verbal expressions of death wish.

If elements of this list constitute a pattern that is worrisome to you, if it seems to you that your kid may be in danger, then *get help now.*

Listen to your youngster. Try to draw him or her into a meaningful talk. *Don't act as if the situation isn't serious.* Get competent professional help immediately. Don't try to do any diagnosing yourself: So many kids who have these symptoms are abusing chemicals and are not suicidal. Don't try to decide which for yourself.

Act now to prevent the worst that could happen.

13

A NATURAL HIGH

OUR ADDICTION

The lives of too many kids in this country are going down the tubes—lives diminished, sometimes demolished, by alcohol and drugs. Chemicals break their bodies, cripple their minds. We know well by now the family ties of the disease: In one out of three families in America, there's a case of alcoholism or drug addiction. One out of every three fourth-graders gives drugs a try. *Fourth-graders!*

Okay, here's the hard part: There are no easy solutions to the problems. We can't just say, "Destroy the cocaine in Peru" or "Burn all the pot in California." Blockading the coast of Florida wouldn't work, nor would having armed guards at all our major airports or even arresting every dealer in the country.

All the measures that can be tried—legal, diplomatic, crime-preventive—haven't been much more than mildly successful.

What can we do about this country's second largest agricultural crop, marijuana? A posse of a million law enforcers might make a dent, but we doubt they could stop it.

Supposing even that we could eradicate the user's supply, what would we do about the oldest drug of all, alcohol? Since man first noticed that the grapes he had stepped on the week before had turned into a nifty concoction that would give him a buzz, the world has pursued the perfect high.

And what about "designer drugs," synthetics that are easy to manufacture in a primitive laboratory and add to the look-alike pills that mimic the chemical action of the most illicit uppers and downers? Even in the pages of our most family-oriented magazines, the message of "take a little something" for everything is plainly advertised.

We are a medicating nation. The market is *us. If there were no market, there would be no problem.*

HELP—AND HOPE

We decided to write this book because, while it gives us enormous satisfaction to help families recover from addiction, we can't reach nearly enough of those in trouble, even within the regional boundaries of our Institute. We want to reach as many parents as we can, as many as this book allows us to, with a message you know well by now: that there *is* hope, and there *is* help, for recovery . . . but it's got to begin with you. If your kid is in trouble, or you think he or she is in trouble, you're the one who has to set the recovery process in motion.

As we told you in our Prologue, helping addictive families fight back is *our* addiction. Nothing in our previous professional or personal lives prepared us for the exhilaration, the natural high, that we get from seeing the recovery process begin to work.

In our hospital detoxification program we work with more and more physicians who see the positive results of our efforts to guide addicted patients—young and old alike—toward chemical freedom. Many of these doctors are participating in the treatment of patients whom, in the past, they would have labeled "untreatable," or "uncooperative," or simply "hopeless."

On occasion patients have arrived in the emergency room asking for help, and their own private physicians hadn't even known there was a chemical problem until the moment these people presented themselves—obviously drunk or high, and satisfying all the criteria associated with addiction.

Remember, adults and adolescents alike can be great con artists—fully capable of hiding their illness, managing to look and act okay until they reach the last stage of addiction.

It is a sad fact that medical school isn't a place where the doctor-to-be can learn much about alcoholism: Of the 120-odd medical schools in this country, only 40 even offer a course in the subject. The same lack of education regarding chemical dependency holds true in schools which teach our other health professions! Now consider *this* fact: On any given day, according to reliable estimates, more than half the hospital beds in the U.S. are occupied by patients who've felt the effects, both directly and indirectly, of what we see as the nation's number-one health problem: drug dependency. From the broken leg of the drunk who was in a car accident, to the overdose of the suicidal adolescent, to the ulcers of the worried spouse of an alcoholic, to the high blood pressure of the adult child of an addicted parent, all are victims of this hidden illness.

But society is finally, *finally* beginning to call for help. And it's our hope that the warnings—on television, over the radio, in newspapers and magazines—will be picked up by members of the health professions. But if they don't respond to those messages, if they continue to think that dealing with drug use and abuse is not their business, then to the shame of these professions, society will turn to those less-trained individuals who are, at least, already doing and showing that they really care.

WHAT IS WORKING NOW?

The kind of effective treatment we described earlier—that is, treating the whole illness: the mental, physical, and spiritual aspects of it—and the concept of treating the whole family as an essential component of the process has successfully changed lives and returned thousands of addicted kids to their families in a state of wellness none of them thought they'd see again. This treatment works.

But we can't stress strongly enough that, barring strong indications to the contrary (such as clinical proof of psychotic behavior or severe depression preceding chemical use), the many problems arising from alcohol and drug use *cannot be properly addressed until the person is chemically free for an extended period.* A surprising number of behavioral disorders disappear when the patient stops drinking or using drugs; being clean and dry is the first, essential step toward recovery.

We are encouraged by the increasing number of health professionals, therapists, legislators, law enforcement officials, and members of the community at large who are recognizing the awful magnitude of addiction in every facet of our society.

Teaching our kids to say no is vital. The growth of Twelve-Step programs—AA, NA, Al-Anon, and Alateen—is heartening, and the emergence of new groups like Al-Anon's Adult Children of Alcoholics has done wonders for millions of us who never knew it was possible to recover from disastrous childhoods.

But, to us, more critical, and more exciting, is the possibility that this book can have a ripple effect on the parents of America—that you and other readers around you will act on the message that prevention is the best medicine, and that prevention begins at home. Positive change can be effected when we are honest enough, and responsible enough, to say, "It begins with me. With us."

The strength to change has to come from each mother, each father, overcoming fear and shame and guilt and denial that there is a problem. It doesn't mean doing it alone. Find help; we've suggested ways. There are professionals out there who are eager to help, eager to listen in a caring, confidential, and nonjudgmental way.

When you find that help, it's your turn to listen. If your kid is diagnosed as addicted, or as a serious abuser of chemicals, and you're advised to get him or her into treatment, please do it. Don't make excuses either to yourself or to your youngster. Don't look around for some "other" kind of help in an effort to postpone the inevitable. Don't say, "Isn't that a bit drastic?"

Have the courage to change: yourself, your kid, your family. For it is in effecting *this* change, now, that our hope for the future lies . . . a refusal on our part to let the illness spread to yet another generation.

AFTERWORD:
OUR DREAM

PREVENTION—AN EARLY WARNING SYSTEM

Both of us have been deeply and personally affected by the disease of alcoholism in our families. We know what happens when addiction becomes a "family member." We know the pain, but we also know the joy of recovery—and we have a dream.

We dream of a world free of the disease of addiction; and to get there we see the need to reach our children. It is through them and future generations that we can provide the "vaccine" of prevention. We dream of reaching these children *before* they are infected. We dream of families becoming whole and of a society that understands.

How do we plan on getting there? On a broad base we know that helping professionals must gain a knowledge of this illness in order to address the problems of fetal alcoholism, family abuse, disruptive behavior, and the various mental and physical problems caused by addiction in the family. Early education of school children must become an essential part of every child's learning experience.

Kids at risk for the multiple problems that come from living in a chemically dependent family need to be identified, and resources to help them must be provided.

One government study identified nine primary needs of children which are often lacking in an alcoholic home:

1. Protection from experiencing or witnessing physical or psychological parental violence.
2. Parental love, support, comfort, and nurture.
3. The experience of forming satisfying emotional relationships with male and female adults.
4. The experience of being respected by family and community.
5. Relief from stress.
6. Attention to problems they may be experiencing.
7. Acceptance by peers and community.
8. The right to seek help.
9. Treatment for problems resulting from unmet needs.

It is our dream that the needs of these children will be met. Some schools and community-based programs as well as treatment facilities are making progress in this direction, but because few alcoholics (less than five percent!) ever get *any* treatment for their addiction, most of their kids remain prisoners of a disease that thrives on secrecy and is perpetuated by ignorance.

When we founded the Van Ost Institute for Family Living, Inc., we were determined that the word *family* was to be an essential ingredient of our programs. We believed that families have the power to make positive changes that can interrupt the legacy of a disease being passed through the generations. One result is that we are establishing a program for young kids of chemically dependent families to supplement those programs already in place for their parents. We want to get them while they're young. It has not been easy for these reasons:

1. Insurance reimbursement for treatment that recognizes the addicted person but ignores the other family members makes financing of these services difficult.
2. There is a lack of therapists in the chemical dependency field who are specifically family oriented.
3. Public funding programs for treatment of children from addicted families is just beginning to be recognized and addressed.

As parents, we believe in the pediatric credo of *prevention* as the true response to the threat of disease. Our dream of a drug-free world depends on how much we provide for the needs of children—it is through them that it can all be accomplished.

To repeat the thought that keeps us on our own natural high: Chemical dependency is the one chronic, progressive disease that, when you recover, leaves you in better health than you were before you got sick.

That goes for you, your kid, and your family.

APPENDIX 1

Family Genogram

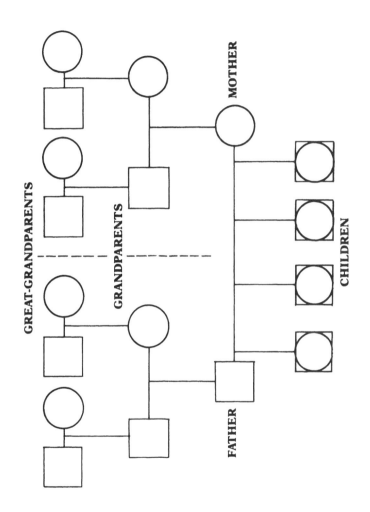

APPENDIX 2

The Survival Roles of Kids In a Chemical Dependent Family

	OUTSIDE BEHAVIOR	FEELINGS	PAYOFF	UNTREATED	TREATED
	What you see OR The visible traits	What you don't see OR The inside story	What the child represents to the family and why they play along	As an adult without having gotten help	As an adult having gotten help
The name of the game OR the mode of survival					
THE FAMILY HERO/ HEROINE or SUPER KID	The little mother; the little man of the family; ALWAYS does what is right; over achiever; over responsible; needs everyone's approval; not much fun	Hurt, inadequate, confusion, guilt, fear, low self esteem, never feels s/he can do enough	Provides self worth to the family—someone to be proud of	Workaholic; never wrong; marry a dependent person; need to control and manipulate; compulsive; can't say no; can't fail	To accept failure; to be able to relax; make good executives; be responsible ONLY for self; OK to say no, enjoy their success

THE SCAPEGOAT or PROBLEM KID	Hostility and defiance; withdrawn, sullen; gets negative attention; won't compete	Hurt and abandoned; anger and rejection; feels totally inadequate; no or low self-esteem	Takes the focus off the real problem—see what s/he's done! Leave me alone.	Alcoholic or addict; unplanned pregnancy; cops; jail; TROUBLE	Recovery; has courage; good under pressure; can see reality; can help others; no trouble; good counselors
THE LOST CHILD or WHERE/WHO IS S/HE?	Loner; daydreamer; solitary rewards; withdrawn; drifts and floats through life; not missed for days; quiet; shy, ignored	Unimportant; not allowed to have feelings; loneliness, hurt and abandoned; defeated and given up; fear	Relief—at least one kid not to worry about	Indecisive; no zest; stays the same; alone or promiscuous; dies early; can't say no	Independent, talented, and creative; imaginative, assertive, and resourceful, successful artists and writers.

	OUTSIDE BEHAVIOR	FEELINGS	PAYOFF	UNTREATED	TREATED
THE FAMILY MASCOT or FAMILY CLOWN	Super cute, immature anything for a laugh or attention; fragile and needful of protection, hyper active, short attention span, learning disabilities, anxious	Low self esteem; terror; lonely, inadequate and unimportant	Comic relief; fun and humor; take heat off the chemically dependent	Compulsive clown; lampshade on head type; can't handle stress; marry a HERO; always on the verge of hysterics	Charming host and person, good company; quick, with good sense of humor; independent and helpful; only funny by personal choice-freedom

From The Johnson Institute, Minn.; The Freedom Institute, NYC; *The Family Trap* by S. Wegscheider

APPENDIX 3

Is There a Problem or Isn't There?
Major and Minor Criteria for Chemical Dependency Diagnosis

The following chart, listing some of the criteria for adolescent chemical dependency, was not designed to be used as a substitute for a complete diagnostic workup by a professional. However, it can provide a system by which a parent can categorize significant WARNING SIGNS to determine the need for referral to experts in the field.

Note that most of the signs are behavioral. The MAJOR CRITERIA are more of the "smoking gun" variety and are more obvious than the MINOR CRITERIA, which, if taken separately out of context, can each be interpreted as "normal" adolescent behavior. It is essential, therefore, that the entire picture be considered—thus, this chart. If, in addition to one MAJOR CRITERIA, three or more MINOR CRITERIA are indicated as being positive, a professional should be consulted for a complete evaluation. Your kid may well be in trouble.

> **ONE MAJOR** CRITERIA
> **PLUS**
> **THREE MINOR** CRITERIA
> **EQUALS**
> PRIMARY DIAGNOSIS OF
> **CHEMICAL DEPENDENCY**
>
> (THE GREATER THE NUMBER
> OF MINOR CRITERIA,
> THE MORE LIKELY THE DIAGNOSIS)

ADOLESCENT "WARNING SIGNS"

1. TWO OCCASIONS OF ACUTE DRUG ABUSE
(Observed by parents, police, alert emergency-room physician or others, i.e., siblings, classmate, teacher.)

2. REGULAR DRUG USE
a) Continuous use in spite of firm no-drug stand by family or physician.
b) Inability to stop in spite of obvious consequences.
c) *Progressive* behavioral changes.
d) Laboratory evidence.

1. DETERIORATION IN SCHOOL PERFORMANCE
a) Erratic school grades and "skipping."
b) Dropping extracurricular activities.
c) Stated loss of interest in academic pursuits.
d) School failure, more frequent skipping, expulsion.
e) Vocal disrespect for teachers.
f) School dropout.

2. DETERIORATION OF FAMILY RELATIONSHIPS
a) Avoidance of family activities.
b) Refusal to do chores.
c) Change in family communications, e.g., refusal to take part in discussions, previous closeness dissipates.
d) Family fights, verbal outbursts, violence or threats of violence toward parents or siblings.
e) Complete rejection of family values.

3. NEGATIVE PERSONALITY CHANGES
a) Moderate "after the fact" lying.
b) Unpredictable mood and attitude swings.
c) "Conning" behavior and expressed feelings of depression.
d) Amotivational behavior, lack of affect.
e) Pathological lying.
f) Severe mental deterioration (memory loss and flashbacks).
g) Paranoia, violent anger and aggression.

4. PHYSICAL CHANGES
a) Frequent sore throats, cough, red eyes.
b) Rebellious dress styles, e.g., rock-beer commercial T-shirts, army jackets, worn jeans, long hair . . . getting messages from the drug/alcohol cultures.
c) Physical deterioration: weight loss, chronic cough, etc.

5. LEGAL PROBLEMS
a) Minor delinquent involvement, steady job with no savings.
b) Police incidents: DWI, stealing, shoplifting, etc.
c) Missing money from purses or coin collections at home, at relatives', or work.
d) Missing or diluted liquor supply from home.

6. CHANGES IN PEER GROUP
   a) Mixed friends (Straight and drug users).
   b) Unexplained phone calls and visits by un-
       familiar friends.
   c.) Change from grade school "straight" friends
       to "losers."

**Modified from "Drugs, Drinking and Adolescents"
by D.I. MacDonald, M.D., F.A. A.P., with the
permission of the author.

Copyright: William C. Van Ost, M.D.,F.A.A.P.,
Co-Founder/Consultant and former Executive Director
THE VAN OST INSTITUTE FOR FAMILY LIVING, INC.
150 East Palisade Avenue, Englewood, NJ 07631-3013

APPENDIX 4

The Twelve Steps of Alcoholics Anonymous

1. We admitted we were powerless over alcohol—that our lives had become unmanageable.
2. Came to believe that a Power greater than ourselves could restore us to sanity.
3. Made a decision to turn our will and our lives over to the care of God, *as we understood Him.*
4. Made a searching and fearless moral inventory of ourselves.
5. Admitted to God, to ourselves, and to another human being the exact nature of our wrongs.
6. Were entirely ready to have God remove all those defects of character.
7. Humbly asked Him to remove our shortcomings.
8. Made a list of all persons we had harmed, and became willing to make amends to them all.
9. Made direct amends to such people wherever possible, except when to do so would injure them or others.
10. Continued to take personal inventory and when we were wrong promptly admitted it.
11. Sought through prayer and meditation to improve our conscious contact with God, *as we understood Him*, praying only for knowledge of His will for us and the power to carry that out.
12. Having had a spiritual awakening as the result of these steps, we tried to carry this message to alcoholics and to practice these principles in all our affairs.

PARENTS: WAS "WARNING SIGNS" HELPFUL?

In order to partially address the second part of its Mission Statement:*"To advance public and professional knowledge of addictive illnesses as treatable disease which can affect the entire family through research and educational activities,"* the Van Ost Institute's Board of Trustees sought and received sufficient funding from generous donors to enable the printing of 10,000 copies of this updated version of "Warning Signs," originally published by Warner Books in 1988 .

Thanks to those good donors and to the assistance with distribution by Dr. Aaron Graham, Bergen County, New Jersey Superintendent of Schools and that of many local public and private school superintendents and parent groups, all 10,000 copies have been distributed at no charge to area parents; particularly targeting those with children who are about to or have just entered fifth grade....the age that a vast majority of our kids start experimenting with alcohol, tobacco and other drugs.

Approximately 14,000 children are now in the fifth grade in our area's public, private and parochial schools. That means that the parents of about 4,000 of our area's 11 and 12 year old children have yet to be been given this educational opportunity to learn what to look for and how to intervene if their kids are already using.

IF THE BOOK WAS HELPFUL, we are asking for your help... The Institute is seeking funding to print more books for distribution to the parents of those 4,000 or more kids who have not yet received a copy. Fully deductible donations to "The Van Ost Institute Book Fund," 150 East Palisade Ave.,Englewood, NJ 07631 would be be most appreciated.

Our nation has a crying need for more **knowledgeable parents.....** the essential keystones to the success of any effort to stop the epidemic growth of addiction problems amongst our children. What parents don't know is hurting us all. Help us, as we try to do something about it.

INDEX